FICTION FORMULA PLOTTING

By

Deborah Chester

Other Books by Deborah Chester

Nonfiction:
FICTION FORMULA PLOTTING
THE FANTASY FICTION FORMULA

Fiction:
REIGN OF SHADOWS
SHADOW WAR
REALM OF LIGHT
THE PEARLS
THE CROWN
THE SWORD
THE RING
THE CHALICE
THE QUEEN'S GAMBIT
THE KING BETRAYED
THE QUEEN'S KNIGHT
THE KING IMPERILED

Writing as Sean Dalton:
SPACE HAWKS
OPERATION PEREGRINE
BEYOND THE VOID
THE ROSTMA LURE
DESTINATION MUTINY
THE SALUKAN GAMBIT

Writing as C. Aubrey Hall:
CRYSTAL BONES
THE CALL OF EIRIAN
MAGE FIRE

TOC

FICTION FORMULA PLOTTING

Introduction

Are you eager to write? Is your mind teeming with characters, settings, and situations, but do you feel confused about how to handle them?

Where should you begin?

What should your characters do first?

How many protagonists should you have?

How do you explain setting and background to readers?

Should your most exciting event happen first or last?

What should go in the middle?

How is the ending constructed?

Such questions—and I could add many more to this sampling—can seem endless. Too many choices and decisions can feel so overwhelming it's easy to become befuddled or even blocked. If this is you, are you tempted to abandon your project completely?

Don't let frustration beat you.

There are ways to combat the confusion. Never let the task of plot development make you doubt yourself or your story premise to the point of giving up.

While the challenges of plotting can tie writers into creative knots, planning decisions made the Fiction Formula way will help you avoid many potential pitfalls, plot holes, and dead ends.

This book and its companion volume of exercises will focus on how to plot commercial genre fiction written according to the principles of classic story

1

design. I call these principles the Fiction Formula. As you gain mastery over the basics, you can then—should you find classic story design too confining—branch out into other types of experimental or even avant-garde forms. That's entirely up to you. There are several styles of writing fiction. Some have mass appeal; others are an acquired taste and attract only a few.

However, classic design has been entertaining western civilization successfully for thousands of years, and it will continue to enthrall readers. The farther away you move from its approach, the smaller your potential audience will become.

While incorporating the writing principles of classic storytelling, the Fiction Formula method is by no means the only way to put a story together; it's simply an approach that's proven to work.

This book will show you how to isolate the most important plot events in your idea and lay out what should happen in your story from start to finish. And although almost every tale you spin has curveballs to throw at you along the way, once you understand the principles of solid plotting you'll be able to handle the unexpected. Even better, you'll be able to turn it to your story's advantage.

In this book, I have organized the chapters systematically, much the way I approach any writing project. But you may dive into any chapter in whatever order suits you best. The companion workbook, *Fiction Formula Plotting Practice,* offers drills, exercises, and checklists to coordinate with each chapter.

Keep in mind that while some genres—such as mysteries and romance—have plot structures unique to them, the same general principles of cohesive, dramatic, enthralling storytelling work for any genre and for any length of fiction whether you're tackling a short story, novella, novel, or series.

Let's begin.

Chapter 1
Defining Plot

Whether you are struck by a bolt of inspiration or your idea comes to you shyly in tiny bits and pieces, it's useful to understand that a collection of incidents or character conversations do not constitute a plot.

A setting—no matter how vividly you've built it in your imagination—does not constitute a plot.

A character—however appealing, cute, and sympathetic—does not constitute a plot.

A group of events lumped together does not constitute a plot.

Impending danger looming over a character does not constitute a plot.

What, then, IS a plot?

In the Fiction Formula approach, plot is defined as **a dramatized accounting of an individual being tested by a force of directed antagonism in a step-by-step struggle that will force the individual through an arc of change.**

Excuse me, *what?*

Indigestible, isn't it? Let's break this working definition into pieces and examine them one at a time for better clarification.

A plot is a dramatized account.

Stop here. Let's expand on this. *Dramatized* means you'll be writing the story action in a series of scenes and their aftermaths, all linked together in a logical progression. Something—a catalyst or launch event—will occur in the opening pages, and as a direct result of it, the next event will happen. As a direct result of *that*, the next event will take place. And so on.

When you dramatize your plot into scenes, you are writing each moment-by-moment event as it happens in story time, without summary.

Alternatively, you can present your story in narrative, but although a great deal of nineteenth and twentieth-century fiction was written in a summarized mode of discourse—including omniscient author intrusion—heavy reliance on narrative changed in the 1970s. Today, most genre fiction is primarily written in scene action that unfolds on the page step by step through a viewpoint character's perspective.

An individual being tested.

Every genre story needs a protagonist, an individual central to the plot. This character's arc of change will come about through the plot events that are designed and chosen to test him or her. If the story is to have much dramatic merit—i.e. readability—it should test the protagonist hard.

In real life, people resist change. They prefer to stay where they are, whether they like their situation or not, because it's familiar and they understand it. Change, you see, brings uncertainty. And people tend naturally to avoid any alteration to their status quo that might bring about the unknown.

But in fiction, we're writing stories about situations chosen or designed to *force* the story protagonist to change. (I'll go deeper into the whys and wherefores in Chapter 7.)

Often the central character is reluctant to move or grow, but that's okay. All the challenges, setbacks, and conflict this character will face in the story will be designed to get at who the protagonist really is—what the protagonist is truly made of. Is this character a hero? Maybe not at the start, but by the end of the story he or she will have become heroic. Or will have gained insight. Or will be able to face a problem from the past. Or will find the courage to apologize or make restitution for a past mistake. Or will become king. Or will find true love. Or will be redeemed in some way.

Change is scary. It's threatening. It's difficult. And, in fiction, it's necessary. Otherwise, we're going to read a story about a character who never unmasks, who solves every problem with ease, and who is—yawn—boring.

The force of antagonism.

When an individual—our protagonist—meets an oppositional force of antagonism, the result is character conflict. Stories need conflict the way our bodies need oxygen. Without conflict, stories wither and die quickly.

You can contrive a random series of dangerous incidents to befall your protagonist. For example, you decide she will narrowly escape a rock avalanche. Then she will be attacked by a puma. Then she must cross a river and the current will be so strong it sweeps her along and nearly drowns her. Then, once she reaches the bank and climbs it, she will stumble into a swarm of biting gnats that try to eat her alive. After that, she'll go into allergic shock from her bites and will be rushed to a hospital by the local park ranger.

Wow. Isn't that an exciting plot?

Nope.

Why not? We've got danger and excitement. Won't that hold a story together?

Well . . . let's just say that a skilled author might contrive a string of such hideous bad luck into a story of sorts. But it can't be sustained plausibly—repeat, *plausibly*—for more than a few pages because these random adventures lack cohesion. They quickly will lose their novelty for a reader. And what's the point anyway?

But if instead of writing "Danielle's Awful Hiking Day" we use the Fiction Formula approach by creating an antagonist for Danielle—an antagonist that's a sentient character with a well-motivated reason for attacking her—then we've generated actual plot.

Let's say that Danielle meets a new co-worker and hits it off with the guy quickly. Danielle finds something elusively familiar about Jonah but can't put her finger on it. She and Jonah seem to have a lot in common, and when Jonah invites Danielle to go hiking with him that weekend, she accepts. Danielle used to hike frequently when she was a teen, but she stopped after her little brother was lost in the woods and never found. And so, while she's enjoying the beautiful scenery, she's also remembering that past tragedy and regretting that she didn't watch out for Buddy the way she should have.

Then, without warning, Jonah shoves Danielle off the trail and she falls into a ravine. She could have died there, but she's only stunned. Half-concussed, she gains her feet and calls out to Jonah for help, but he starts a small avalanche of rocks crashing down on her, and she must run for her life. Then Jonah starts shooting at Danielle, who dives into the river at the bottom of the ravine. The current is very strong, and Danielle is weakened by her injuries. She nearly drowns but finally climbs onto the opposite bank. Jonah shoots at her again, this time wounding her grievously. Jonah leaves Danielle for dead, but with the last of her strength she finds one weak signal bar on her cell phone and manages to call for help, bringing a park ranger who rushes her to a hospital.

A reader can be wondering *why, why, why* throughout Danielle's ordeal, but Jonah's antagonism—although unexplained at this stage—creates an exciting escalation of trouble for her and will probably hook readers into continuing the story to find out what lies behind his villainous behavior. Is he really the long-lost brother Buddy? Does he blame Danielle for what happened to him? Is he after revenge? Readers will wonder that, and if he isn't Buddy after all, then there are more plot twists to come.

Step-by-step struggle.

Now, as we continue through our definition of plot, we're reaching the heart and soul of it: conflict. When you set up a directly opposed antagonist, strife between protagonist and antagonist is inevitable. And if you dramatize that struggle, the scene action happens step by step in a logical, plausible cause-and-effect progression of events. Writing this way saves you from having to string an assortment of disconnected incidents together.

Constructing scenes by the Fiction Formula approach makes them focused, clear, and easy for readers to follow. When you build scenes and their reactions this way, figuring out what will happen next is simple. There's no need to strain for ideas or contrive a series of disconnected events. Scenes written in accordance with basic writing principles will keep your story on track.

The protagonist's arc of change.

Forcing the protagonist through an arc of change is what commercial fiction is all about. Throughout a story, the plot events and the antagonist are testing the protagonist to see what makes her tick. Is she brave and resourceful? Will she find the inner strength to withstand what's thrown at her? Will she risk her life to save her child, or will she be able finally to let go of former self-doubts and trust in a new relationship?

In real life, many people slide along between home and job, keeping themselves out of trouble by never making waves, never taking risks, never growing as individuals because they avoid challenges and difficulties. They're called prudent by some and stodgy by others, but either way they cruise through life and survive.

But realistic people do not make vivid characters. They won't come to life within the pages of a short story or a book. Instead, characters are designed to be anything but realistic. While some of them are intrepid and full of pluck from page one, others are pushed by story circumstances into a new life or venture, one full of risks and scary situations. Frodo Baggins in J.R.R. Tolkien's *The Lord of the Rings* did *not* want to leave the comfort of his hearth, and yet he was swept out into an enormous adventure that tested him to the very limits of his strength, courage, and endurance. That test made a hero of him.

Now, permit me to repeat my working definition as follows:

Plot is a dramatized accounting of an individual being tested by a force of directed antagonism in a step-by-step struggle that will force the individual through an arc of change.

Does it make better sense to you now? Has your understanding of what plot is, and is not, gained clarity?

[For exercises in developing a preliminary plot premise, see Chapter 1 in *Fiction Formula Plotting Practice.*]

Chapter 2
Idea Development

Some writers have no difficulty in putting together a plot within a few minutes. Others struggle for days or weeks, winding themselves into a tangle of confusing images, bits of dialogue, and an unruly cast of characters they can't seem to find parts for. And still others sit blankly, staring at their computer screens in hopes that inspiration will eventually strike.

One of my favorite "writer" films is the 1987 Billy Crystal comedy, *Throw Mama from the Train*. The hero, angry at his ex-wife for having stolen his novel, is too upset to write. Consequently, he sits at his typewriter day after day, searching for the perfect adjective and unable to complete the opening sentence for his next work of fiction.

The Fiction Formula approach does not rely on inspiration. It welcomes it when it drops by, of course. Certainly, inspiration can enhance certain story events already outlined or even solve a plot problem or two along the way, but it does not always arrive on time, if at all.

When you understand classic story design and how its writing principles fit together to form a story, then plotting a new idea becomes a matter of putting those principles to work.

However, how is a new idea even generated? Creative people never know what's going to spark fire in their imaginations. When it ignites, we love that sizzle, don't we? It's a rush of excitement that urges us to get started.

But again, if you rely only on the spark, what do you do when it fizzles or doesn't come at all?

Does that mean your idea is no good?

Not at all. It means you'll have to work harder to put your story together.

A Fiction Formula writer understands that sometimes it's necessary to put in a lot of effort to generate a story idea, develop it, and test it before inspiration strikes.

Brainstorming

If you haven't been planning your book since eighth grade or if you haven't awakened from a dream that's awarded you with a fabulous idea, then you'll probably have to try some brainstorming. Whether you do it with a group of buddies, one trusted friend, or by yourself doesn't matter.

If you bounce ideas off others, you need to be sure you're comfortable with them. Ideally you want a group of writers at your level of expertise, and the group should be small and committed to helping each other—not present to tear anyone down or steal ideas discussed in the session. If you're meeting with a buddy, then that individual should be a writer also or someone who reads avidly enough to have a solid sense of story. Avoid brainstorming with anyone with poor story sense or the desire to please you by agreeing with anything you say.

Whether it's an all-day plotting fest, a lunch, or an evening's chat, sharing ideas can produce the excitement that will send you rushing to your keyboard. At this stage, however, you aren't ready to write. Hold back.

It's also important when brainstorming to avoid censoring yourself too harshly or overthinking. Go with your gut reactions: "I like that a lot! Wait! Let me jot it down." Or, "No! What are you thinking? My hero Beauregard would *never* do that."

Let ideas and suggestions flow. When they get too crazy, stop for a while. Make sure you take notes. Later you'll want to mull them over, keeping whatever appeals to you—even if you don't know why—and rejecting anything that doesn't.

You can also brainstorm alone. Set aside all distractions, and silence your phone. Then, in the quiet, write down anything that comes to you: the name of a town, a setting, a passage of description, an exchange of dialogue, the image of an axe for whatever reason, colors, whatever's swirling through your mind.

It also helps to collect images and photos that inspire you or seem to fit the setting you're building. Then spend some time pondering them and letting ideas flow.

When I am thinking in solitude, I like to sift through whatever I already have. At this stage, I'm committed to nothing. I ask myself questions such as these: Do I like it? Who is my primary character? Are any names coming to mind? Do I have faces yet to go with the names?

Maybe I'm fascinated by a strong personality trait or a tag I can assign to my star character.

Or it could be that I have a glimmer of a scene in mind. Can I string any other scenes to it? What's at stake in it? What will be the consequences of it?

None of this is permanent at this stage. I'm chiseling nothing in stone. Anything can be erased. In fact, what I eventually write may diverge considerably from what I'm intending at this point.

The result of brainstorming should be growth of the premise. Try to end a session with at least six to fifteen events in mind. You'll need more than this, of course, to flesh out a novel, but don't worry about that yet. You have plenty to do right now, and you aren't ready to write.

In this phase, I don't bother to organize my notebook or computer file. I'm trying to stay completely in the creative hemisphere of my brain. I'm not ready to be objective and editorial yet. The point of my notes isn't to be rigid and controlled but instead to serve as a tangible idea receptacle.

Years ago, I used to believe that the best aspects of a good idea when it's growing and taking shape in one's mind wouldn't be forgotten, and the worst elements would be discarded anyway. So why bother with notes? However, experience has taught me there's nothing more maddening than to have a terrific idea nugget slip away, forgotten, despite its being exactly the detail most needed.

I find that I can relax more if I'm writing things down. It aids my creative process. It doesn't mean that I'll use or adhere to any of what goes into the pages or file. But what seems brilliant in my mind can become suddenly lame on the page. When that happens, such a change in perception is useful to me. If it's brilliant in my mind and seems darned good also on the page, then hurray! That's even better.

Although I tend to resist early organization— although later it's very useful—if you find the process of making lists and plopping them into document files helpful in sifting through your ideas, then use it. Whatever works best for you is what you should do. Just remember that if ideas stay only in your head, they will always seem better than they are.

And the first key test of any idea or premise is whether it can survive being written down.

Another factor in useful brainstorming is to play the "what if" game. What if my character goes to China? What if the ceiling in the house collapses? What if zombies rise from the town's cemetery and start prowling?

Once you've selected your favorites from a "what if" session, flip them over again. What if my character *doesn't* go to China? What if she ends up in North Africa by mistake? What if the house's ceiling *doesn't* collapse? What if the floor crumbles instead? What if there aren't zombies *leaving* the cemetery? What if a supernatural creature is seeking refuge there instead? And what might that creature be? Someone—or something—in trouble? What could jeopardize a being that's magical or immortal? What's happened? Why is this character seeking a hiding place or sanctuary? What's after it? Why?

See how it begins to work?

Furthermore, you never need accept the first idea that pops into your head. You should feel free to flip ideas, invert them, tweak them, play with them, or even reject them if they stray too far afield. Keep in mind that while your first idea might be a good one, it might be also a stereotypical cliché.

Plot Lists

Once I've done a few brainstorming sessions or have been examining whatever is growing in my imagination, the result is several solid plot events that I will probably use. They can be scene fragments or entire scenes. But now that promising events and incidents are shaping up and evolving, I want to organize them.

I find it useful to settle in a quiet spot and pull together all my notes on potential events that might fit into my story.

I don't edit too strictly yet. I'm weighing and evaluating what I have so far in terms of where each event might fall into the plot's progression. Most importantly, I want to consider what I can use to kick off the story. Some of you know this as the "inciting incident." I usually refer to it as the catalyst or the change with consequences. As I audition each potential first event, I'm asking myself the following questions:

Is this exciting enough dramatically to launch a story?

Can it both launch the story and introduce my protagonist at the same time?

Does it bring change with consequences that can't plausibly be ignored by the characters involved?

Do I have anything better?

Should this event happen later in the story?

As soon as I can narrow down the opening event to one or two alternatives, I want to generate a new list based on each optional first event. From these different starting points, what would plausibly happen next? And then what? And so on. Usually I don't have to go far before I know which opening event I'll choose.

You'll need maybe three or four events for a short story and roughly twenty for a novel of 60,000-75,000 words. If your list contains more than twenty events, then perhaps you're focusing too minutely on minor incidents or else you're planning an 80,000- to 95,000-word manuscript.

There's no hard and fast rule about the number of events. I'm simply offering you a general guideline that will help you evaluate whether you've over-plotted or under-plotted.

The Working Outline

Now it's time to pull your plot into a chronological list, outline, or synopsis. It's time to commit yourself somewhat. At this point, you're only engaged; it's not yet a binding marriage. You can still back out if your plot premise fails its tests. However, don't start testing yet. Look at your list of possible plot events and satisfy yourself that they're in a logical, not random, order. Then write a plot synopsis.

This means to summarize what will happen in your story from start to finish. Limit yourself to no more than ten double-spaced pages, and don't squinch down the font to cheat. If you exceed ten pages, you're probably elaborating too much on setting or character description, or else you're dwelling too long on each event. Shorten until you're within the ten-page length. If a critical event has been left out, check your explanations and description again. Sacrifice them to keep your event.

This is the preliminary version of what will become a working synopsis or outline.

Are you hesitant to do this? After all, it's boring! It's hard! It makes your exciting idea seem flat and lifeless. On top of that, ten pages is so arbitrary.

Stop whining!

Yes, it's necessary. And, no, you're not yet ready to write the actual story.

Instead, you're ready to test your plot.

[See Chapter 2 in *Fiction Formula Plotting Practice* for exercises in generating ideas.]

Chapter 3
Testing Premise

It's exciting to finally have a string of plot events, to feel like your story is taking shape. It's glorious to burn so intensely to start writing you feel you'll die if you can't start soon.

If your emotions are this engaged, that's an excellent sign. Impatience is great, provided you continue to control it.

Fiction Formula plotting means having the intestinal fortitude to face any potential plot problems at the start and plug plot holes before they suck your entire project into disaster.

I know it's agonizing to want to write your story so much you're afraid it will fade if you don't start immediately. I also know how easy it is to ignore weak areas, vague portions, and trouble spots you'd rather not think about. It can be so tempting to use denial to maintain your passion for a project.

But consider how much more heartbreaking it is to write on that initial wave of impatience, only to hit a dead end at page 30, or page 50, or—agony—page 150. And when you hit that dead end, you're going to stop and probably throw everything away. Lost pages. Lost time. Total frustration.

It is so much better to test your story premise the *easy* way—while it's still an idea, still an outline—instead of the *hard* way of writing blindly in hopes you'll stumble somehow through a plot from start to finish.

If you're afraid to test your plot, that indicates you know it's weak and you're simply guarding it.

Saving what's weak is *not* the Fiction Formula way.

Writing what's strong *is*.

When you're crafting a plausible, solid plot, you'll find yourself working with confidence instead of uncertainty. The difference is amazing.

Now, in evaluating your premise, you need to consider plausibility, built-in conflict, and originality. Let's examine them one at a time.

Plausibility

Logical cause-and-effect plotting stems from setting up several factors that will contribute to the story in a rational, believable way.

At any given time, your story should withstand the following questions:

In the circumstances, is my character's action logical?

Is my character's action motivated correctly?

Will the consequences of my character's action generate the result I want?

Logic means there is a reason for an action taken, not just a random impulse. Your characters and their story situation should connect to each other. One action dictates another that dictates another, and so on.

When there is a car crash, investigators immediately examine the scene to find out what happened and what caused it to happen. Police and insurance adjustors must determine this to assign blame and charge the driver at fault so that the appropriate insurance policy will pay repair costs.

Motivation needs to govern the behavior of your characters, and readers need to know and understand that motivation. Without the *why* behind what your characters say and do, story events will seem random. Even worse, they will stop making sense.

Naturally in fiction, you can have anything happen that you wish, but only if it's motivated plausibly and if it connects to other events happening in the story.

Consequences should never be overlooked. Your characters don't operate in vacuums. What they do should carry results. What they say should lead to something else. In real life—especially if we are but a tiny corporate cog slaving in a gray cubicle—we don't always see the results of our efforts. But fiction is ordered differently than the way real life happens.

Take the time to put yourself in your protagonist's head. Think about the events you're planning. Are your character's actions rational? Would anyone really do what you're intending your protagonist to do? Sometimes, in the frothy urgency of cooking up a storyline, we can lose reasonable perspective.

For example, if your protagonist suddenly pulls a gun from her purse and threatens her roommate who hasn't paid her share of the rent, that may seem exciting in a superficial way. It may seem to give your hero Esmeralda a "take-action" persona, but is it plausible that she would react so extremely? Is her action justified by what's at stake?

How many ordinary women carry pistols in their handbags? To justify the gun's presence at all, Esmeralda needs a reason for carrying a weapon, and a reason beyond her trouble collecting rent money. That means you need to think about her background. What, in her past, has driven her to own a weapon? Because regardless of what you see on television, most citizens—especially women—do not carry concealed weapons. Do I know women that do? Yes. Several. One owns a jewelry store and works alone. One runs a bail bond business. One—a local television celebrity—has been threatened by a stalker. One lives on a remote farm about sixty miles from the nearest town and must drive past meth operations on her way to and from home. Each of these women has a valid reason for having purchased a handgun and obtained a permit for it. But their circumstances are special rather than ordinary.

Furthermore, handguns are expensive. They're heavy. (If you think a woman's wallet, phone, and makeup bag weigh down her purse, add a few pounds of weaponry and ammo to the load.) Can Esmeralda fit a spare clip in her fashionable Kate Spade bag along with the Glock? To obtain a permit to carry a handgun, was Esmeralda required to take lessons from a certified instructor at a shooting range? Or have you decided that Esmeralda will carry an illegal gun? Again, why? How and where did she get it?

When your protagonist Esmeralda loses her temper with her flaky roommate and draws a weapon, is that action justified in terms of what's at stake? Is the rent worth possibly shooting an unarmed roommate and going to jail for attempted manslaughter?

What seemed exciting initially has—after due thought—become ludicrous.

If the protagonist and her roomie are merely arguing over who should pay the rent this month, a gun is a worthless prop. It doesn't fit the story circumstances, and it isn't going to plausibly solve the protagonist's problem.

Granted, *if* Esmeralda's cousin insisted she keep his handgun for the weekend because he picked it up after witnessing an altercation between thugs in an alley and now he's afraid to turn it into the police and plans to throw it away soon, and *if* Esmeralda doesn't *want* the gun, even for a day, and *if*—while arguing with her roomie—she inadvertently spills the contents of her purse and the gun falls out and the flaky roomie thinks Esmeralda is going to threaten her with it, and *if* Miss Flake calls the cops, and *if* Esmeralda has to then hide it or explain where she got it, and *if* you're writing a comedy, then you could make this farcical scenario work.

But you have to think through it and supply logic—however goofy—motivation, and consequences.

Built-in Conflict

Generating enough conflict to sustain a story is a challenge for any writer, whether a beginner or a seasoned veteran. Genre fiction thrives on conflict. It's how characters are tested. Without conflict, story suspense cannot be built. Without conflict, the story's outcome is never in question. Without conflict, characters cannot grow and achieve their destiny—or devolve into someone twisted and hollow, as Michael Corleone does in Mario Puzo's *The Godfather*.

Most importantly, without conflict the protagonist cannot achieve change, and poetic justice cannot be dispensed in the story's climax.

Conflict is so vital to story that it comprises 95-98% of scene content. Conflict is what dramatizes a plot event. It is what moves a story forward. It is what keeps a story intriguing to readers.

Without it—and without enough of it—the story will fade and die, just as our bodies are dependent on blood, and enough of it, to live.

We have two sources of conflict to draw on in writing a story. One source is the obvious one between protagonist and antagonist. If their objectives are directly opposed, for strong reasons, they will clash again and again.

The other source of conflict can come from the situation itself. This built-in conflict is a guarantee of discord and disagreement.

Therefore, exactly what is your story situation?

Is your protagonist doing well and holding down a good job? Is he in a stable relationship? Does he live in a safe neighborhood, where kids ride bikes on the sidewalk and people sit on their front porches in the evenings and wave to those walking past? Is his sister happily married? Are his parents healthy and enjoying their retirement?

This example is pleasant but lacks built-in conflict. There's no problem in the situation. All is calm, peaceful, safe, and secure.

That's wonderful in real life, but fiction needs danger, excitement, suspense, and thrills. Fiction needs trouble, and trouble should be a catalyst, a problematic situation, an unknown factor, a rough setting, a change in the status quo with dire consequences.

When you place your protagonist in a safe situation lacking any built-in conflict, you are making your job harder.

It means that trouble will be generated entirely from the actions of an antagonist. There's nothing wrong with this approach. In fact, it works well in sudden-terror stories where the safety of the protagonist is abruptly threatened without warning. Just realize that you are starting from ground zero and should understand the challenges ahead of you.

On the other hand, if you add to the difficulties between the protagonist and antagonist by putting them in a stressful, dangerous, or discordant environment, doing so will exacerbate trouble and intensify their conflict.

While built-in conflict doesn't have to mean setting your story in a battlefield or outer space, it does mean you can take advantage of all sorts of places and relationships. Sibling rivalry for an inheritance, politics within a hospital, two lawyers competing for one partnership at their firm, a loveless marriage, a police precinct, contestants on a cooking show, or a child dying of leukemia are all sample situations fraught with pressure, angst, bitterness, misery, stress, and disagreement. They can be just as compelling as an urban fantasy story dealing with an outbreak of spell pestilence and rabid fairies preying on mortal suburbia.

Originality

Okay, this is the tough one that challenges not just your skill, but your talent. After all, given that there are said to be maybe six dramatic plots out there, and they've all been done forever ago, what chance does a modern-day author have of being original? Is anyone even trying?

Well, sure. Every day. Or we wouldn't have the Harry Potter series, or the Lemony Snicket series, or the Honor Harrington series, or the Jack Reacher series, or the Harry Dresden series, or *The Godfather* trilogy, or the Miss Julia series, or the Precious Ramotswe series, or *The Hobbit*.

The key to originality lies in a couple of factors. The first is knowing your genre. What are its tropes? What are its clichés? What is worn out? What is still going strong? What do readers love most about it? What are they tired of? What attracted you to that genre—and the answer had better not be, *because I can make a lot of money writing it.*

If you've read three novels in a particular genre, you don't know that field. If you've read fifty, you're beginning to understand it. If you've read a hundred, then good for you. Read some of the foundation stories of a popular genre, and read the newest stories within it so that you can mark how the genre has evolved and changed. For example, romance novels of the 1980s are not the same as those written today. Mysteries from the Golden Age between the two world wars feature a different style of sleuth and murder investigation than what's offered now. Poirot's little gray cells have morphed into graphically depicted autopsies and descriptions of the maggots that clean skulls for forensics teams.

Let's say that you want to write for children. Maybe several years ago you consumed all the beloved classics in your library's juvenile section so you feel you are more than well acquainted with *Johnny Tremaine, Little House on the Prairie,* and *Anne of Green Gables.* But have you read the new, current offerings? If not, then the genre will surprise you with its pacing, violence, and profanity.

Think about what draws you to a genre. What makes you love it? Or what do you feel is missing from it? What would you like to see in an urban fantasy story, for instance, that hasn't been done before?

Look through reviews of books in your targeted genre. What are the critics saying? What are readers saying? Do they contradict each other? What's your opinion? What could you do better?

The second factor in being original is understanding that you don't have to invent something the world has never seen before. It's unnecessary to throw out the wheel and invent a dazzling replacement.

Instead, take your knowledge, understanding, and love for your chosen genre and add one new element. Create a combination or fusion that hasn't been done before or hasn't yet been written to death.

Jim Butcher didn't originate the snarky loner protagonist of the urban fantasy genre. But he understood the genre was a fusion of magic with noir, and so he designed a private investigator (in the noir tradition) that was also a wizard (in the fantasy tradition). That combination, when the series began, was new and different.

J.K. Rowling combined the trials and tribulations of boarding school life with magic training. Perhaps she wasn't the very first individual to do so in a story, but her version is certainly the one with the most charm and verve. Her vivid, enchanting world serves up settings and details that pop off the page.

Charlaine Harris has combined fantasy, mystery, and humor in her stories about telepathic Sookie Stackhouse.

Alexander McCall Smith created a gentle series about an intrepid, kind-hearted, clear-thinking, philosophical woman in Botswana that has the courage to start the first ladies' detective agency in her community. Precious Ramotswe is anything but hard-boiled, and her cases are simple ones; she closes her investigations through an understanding of human nature and deductive reasoning. A woman detective isn't new, but one in Botswana is an original combination.

[See Chapter 3 of *Fiction Formula Plotting Practice* for exercises that will generate plausibility in your story ideas.]

Chapter 4
The SPOOC

If your premise has survived the tests of plausibility, built-in conflict, and originality, and if it is a bit battered but still mostly intact, then it's time to stretch it on the SPOOC framework and see how it fits.

Some of my students loathe the SPOOC. They resist and dodge using it just as a yearling colt fights the bridle. I'll confess that when I was a student and trying to learn it, I dreaded dealing with it, too.

This test takes no prisoners. It is the most effective plotting tool I've encountered, and it will immediately pinpoint the weaknesses of an idea quicker than anything else I've tried.

When your plot is weak—or your thinking is fuzzy—you'll find it difficult, if not impossible, to generate a SPOOC correctly. That's never the SPOOC's fault. It's yours.

Face it.

Fix it.

Now, for those of you who are wondering what in the world is a SPOOC, it's simply an acronym for a plot template as follows:

SITUATION:

PROTAGONIST:

OBJECTIVE:

OPPONENT:

CLIMAX:

Don't panic at the idea of shrinking your fabulous, imaginative, exciting, complex plot idea down to these five skimpy elements. It can be done, and it works for novels as well as short stories.

But, but, but—yes, I can hear the sputters of protest from here—surely Jane Austen never had to put up with this for her fine collection of work.

Oh, yeah? No, she didn't know about the SPOOC specifically, but instinctively and naturally she utilized the writing principles it represents.

Let's try it with *Pride and Prejudice.*

SITUATION: With only a skimpy dowry,
PROTAGONIST: Elizabeth
OBJECTIVE: seeks a husband.
But can she become engaged when
OPPONENT: the odious Mr. Darcy, the last man she could ever be compelled to marry,
CLIMAX: turns out to be the man she really loves?

But, but, but—yes, I hear the sputters again. I've barely scratched the surface, haven't I? I can hear these shouts: what about Lydia? And Jane? What about Mr. Wickham? And Mr. Collins? What about Lady Catherine?

Each of those characters represents a subplot of the novel. And each novel subplot needs to be tested also by a SPOOC.

A novel is a long, intricate cloth woven of many elements. Find your central thread first. That is the main plot, the most important one. I've outlined it for you in the above example.

Then select your subplots: Elizabeth versus Mr. Wickham; Darcy versus Wickham; Elizabeth versus Lady Catherine; and so on.

Writers often entangle themselves in Gordian knots of confusion by trying to cram central plot and several subplots together into a single SPOOC. Instead, take it one at a time.

Doing so will help you clarify what your central plotline is. Which one is next important, which comes after it, etc. There should be a hierarchy among your various plotlines.

I'll repeat that writing principle: **In novels, there should be a hierarchy of importance among the various plotlines.**

They are not all equal in value. They should not all receive equal attention.

I know that this writing principle flies against the current trend in young adult fiction of establishing two protagonists and alternating chapters between them equally, so that both characters have the same level of importance and each receives the same number of viewpoint chapters.

This is most often seen with dual protagonists of different genders, and it satisfies a present-day agenda to share story equally. There are positives to this practice, of course.

One positive is that male and female genders are represented for readers to identify with. Neither character is playing second fiddle to the other. No one is being left behind or missing a chance to star. Action and excitement can be kept "up-tempo." The double-helix storyline *seems* to offer extra punch and more complexity.

But there are negatives as well. The first is that this construction violates a writing principle—that of a primary central storyline with a hierarchy of subplots to follow—in favor of a trending social agenda. The agenda means well, but it fights story construction and creates a phony overlay that causes writer headaches—and potential reader disappointment—at the story's conclusion. The double—or multiple—protagonist trend muddles the central story question, and again this creates problems in writing an effective, emotionally satisfying climax. In the back and forth switch of viewpoints between each chapter, the construction becomes predictable, and predictability dulls a story. I call it the "metronome effect." Tick-tock, tick-tock, tick-tock, and thus the book develops a split focus. And—as I will explain further in Chapters 13 and 14—a split focus makes it very hard to write an effective ending.

For writers, the current solution to these construction problems too frequently has become the tendency to toss aside an ending altogether. Or at least abbreviate it in favor of hooking readers instead into buying the next book in a series. This tactic saves writers who don't know how to deal with a plot they can't wrap up. It satisfies publishers who foresee a solid line-up of future sales. However, it frustrates readers who feel cheated and manipulated by such a blatantly commercial trick.

The Fiction Formula would rather make readers happy than annoy them. Instead of tricking readers, it would rather entice them into buying the next book because they enjoyed the first one. The Fiction Formula would rather deliver a truly satisfying, exciting finish instead of leaving readers disappointed by missing emotional catharsis or a lack of poetic justice. The Fiction Formula wants to make worthwhile a reader's investment of money, time, and emotional involvement.

Now, in getting back to the SPOOC, take care that you don't omit the template labels. My students frequently try this tactic when they are resisting mastering the SPOOC. It's rebellion against a plotting discipline that's always much harder to do than it seems, and the result is that they often skip some of the five elements and hope I won't notice. Yet each element is vital and intrinsic to the success of a plot, and the absence of any of them stands out like werewolf eyes glowing through London fog.

The most common omission made by my students is the opponent. For whatever reason, this character role is increasingly overlooked or forgotten. And it is a fatal error.

I've already addressed the need for an antagonist in Chapter 1. I will reiterate it here. Without an antagonist or opponent directly opposed to your protagonist, your story is over as soon as it begins. Without an opponent, there's no doubt as to the outcome. The problem will be solved quickly and easily. Therefore, the stronger the foe the stronger your story will be.

Consider the villain in Sabaa Tahir's *An Ember in the Ashes,* published in 2015. Sadistic and cruel, the Commandant stands out among the cast of characters for her brutality, ruthlessness, and intelligence. Without her, the story would be much less focused or compelling.

The second most common omission within the SPOOC is that of the protagonist's goal. It isn't enough just to create a character and have that individual exist. What is the protagonist doing at the start and intending to do next? Without a specific objective to guide a story, where will it go? And how can a goal-less plot be shaped?

The third major error that can occur is a failure to connect the story situation with the protagonist's goal.

In other words, the *situation* constitutes a problem for the protagonist, some type of trouble that must be dealt with and solved. Therefore, the protagonist's *objective* should be the solving of the situation.

That in turn dictates that the *opponent* should be focused on hindering, thwarting, resisting, or blocking *whatever the protagonist seeks to accomplish.*

Let's repeat this for emphasis: **the opponent should focus on hindering, thwarting, resisting, or blocking *whatever the protagonist seeks to accomplish.***

Often, plots go awry because a writer sets up a goal for the protagonist and a goal for the antagonist, but they lack a connection. When this happens, the plot can never come together without extensive writer contrivance. Even then, it may not work.

On the other hand, if the two goals definitively oppose each other, then the plot will almost write itself.

As for the final element within the SPOOC, the climax is where struggle between protagonist and antagonist comes to a head. It is, in effect, a crisis. It will be a calamity or the imminent threat of one. Often, the stakes are twisted even higher when the antagonist brings about what the protagonist most fears or dreads. This, in turn, forces the protagonist into the final step in his or her arc of change. Their showdown will answer the story question which is, *will the protagonist solve his or her problem? Yes or no?* If you avoid writing this major confrontation, you will not resolve your story to any reader's satisfaction.

[Study the SPOOC examples and explanation in Chapter 4 of *Fiction Formula Plotting Practice* before attempting to write your own.]

Chapter 5
A Plotting Template

At this stage, let's examine how to draw a logical, step-by-step plot from a viable SPOOC. Study the following example as it unfolds chronologically through story progression.

SPOOC

SITUATION: After discovering that evil gnomes have infested the backyard of his new house,

PROTAGONIST: George Rehnquist

OBJECTIVE: wants to drive out the pests.

But can he eradicate the infestation permanently when

OPPONENT: Urk, leader of the gnomes,

CLIMAX: orders a horde of gnomes and their allies—the gremlins—to swarm George's property?

Plotting Outline

Story Step 1—George must discover the problem on page 1, certainly by page 2, and form the immediate intention of removing the gnomes.

Story Step 2—As soon as George takes his first action toward achieving this intention—perhaps he buys a load of soil and starts filling in the gnome holes—a gnome antagonist will resist.

Story Step 3—Urk is irate about a shovelful of dirt dumped in his face, and he will pop up and throw rocks at George. He might even grab George's shovel and take it away from George, pulling it underground.

Story Step 4—George can buy another shovel, but perhaps he sees the futility of that so instead he purchases gnome repellant and sprinkles the pellets down the holes.

Story Step 5—Urk retaliates by leaving his hole and biting George's ankles until George is driven into the house.

Story Step 6—Urk now posts members of his family to guard the backyard, refusing to let George go outside.

Story Step 7—George hires a wizard to cast a repudiation spell over the yard, but the wizard is old and cranky. When he arrives, and sees how many gnomes there are, he ups his price.

Story Step 8—George argues with the wizard, and finally obtains his spell at a slightly reduced cost, but the wizard warns him that because there are so many gnomes the spell will not last more than twenty-four hours—less if it rains. And it rains that night. (Bad weather, aka adversity, creates bad luck for George on top of the conflict.)

Story Step 9—George goes outside the next morning—not realizing rain has washed off the spell—and finds himself confronted by not only all the angry gnomes of Urk's family, but also a horde of gremlins.

Story Step 10—They surround George, cutting him off before he can retreat inside his house. They carry him underground where he is thrown at Urk's hairy feet.

Story Step 11—Urk offers George an ultimatum.

Story Step 12—George realizes the gnomes might be useful in tilling up his vegetable patch and feeding the roots of his roses, and he works out a compromise. He learns that gnomes aren't so bad, and the gnomes discover that if they will agree to dig fewer holes and cultivate the tomatoes, they can all co-exist happily together.

THE END

Are these twelve silly steps of a silly plot scenario sufficient to fill a novel? No. How many plot events did I suggest in Chapter 1? That's right, about twenty. Therefore, this example would suit a novella.

How, then, to double the number of events and expand it into a book? Let's start by adding a subplot involving George and his family. Perhaps one of his children has made friends with a gnome, unaware of how invasive they are. Suppose small Danny has shared his Snickers candy bar with the young gnome, and Fria, hoping for more treats, follows Danny home. Perhaps Fria is Urk's daughter and heir. At some point, Urk might find out about the forbidden friendship. Perhaps Danny and Fria even try to stop the battle, and end up making their fathers' mutual enmity worse.

If the story is to be compressed instead into a short story, then much of it should be cut. For example, have Urk already living in George's backyard when the story opens. The infestation would involve only Urk's immediate family, say a half-dozen gnomes or so, and most of them would stay unnamed in the background.

We would keep Steps 1 and 2, but skip everything until Steps 11 and 12 when George is abducted.

Remember that plot is flexible. It can be expanded or shrunk, as needed, providing you follow the essential writing principles. Plot—whatever its length—should remain logical, plausible, and dramatically valid in testing the protagonist through conflict against a direct opponent.

We don't lengthen a story by padding it with dull passages of description. And we shouldn't load it with a thousand years' worth of your fantasy world's history, philosophy, and magical systems.

We don't shorten a story by chopping off the climax. Neither do we preserve a rambling, too-long story opening at the expense of writing an exciting, fully developed resolution.

[Chapter 5 in *Fiction Formula Plotting Practice* will guide you further in setting up a step-by-step working outline.]

Chapter 6
Involve Your Characters

Do you know any individuals who spend considerable amounts of energy arguing what's more important: plot over character, or character over plot? I've read claims that all plot derives from character and I've encountered criticisms that insist genre fiction favors plot to the point of shortchanging character. Who's right? Is plot paramount? Or is plot just a four-letter word?

The answer is, of course, balance. Plot is important, and it should be. Anytime I attend a literary party and overhear some haughty intellectual sneering at plot as a concept that's hackneyed and useless, I back away. The weak, meandering type of story that I refer to jokingly as a "plotless wonder" had better offer some darned good setting, characterization, and/or insight into human nature to make up for a lack of action. Are there such books? Of course! And some of them are wonderful.

Consider the novel *Jane Eyre*. It follows Jane from the orphanage to her post as governess in the Rochester household. Is there a great deal of high action? Any galloping horses? Any kidnappings? Anyone fighting a duel in the library at midnight? No, nothing like that. I guess the madwoman setting fire to the house is probably the high point of action. But most of the time Jane is going about her duties and trying hard not to fall in love with Mr. Rochester. Does this make the book dull or boring? Not at all. The development of the love story, the growing bond between Jane and Rochester, and Jane's inner arc of change all serve to make this novel compelling and universal.

In romance stories, the focus is on the development of an emotional bond between the two principal players. Therefore, within the modern romance genre, a story event can be comprised of the couple's eyes meeting across a room with new understanding. The story has made progress because their relationship has moved to a different phase. This kind of plot serves up quiet movement that sometimes becomes obscured by the emotions of the characters or the charm of the setting. Yet there is plot.

From time to time, Turner Classic Movies will run features on famous actors or directors as filler material between airing the films. One such filler is centered on accomplished Hollywood director Vicente Minelli. According to the anecdote, Minelli approached studio head Jack Warner about directing a script called *Meet Me in St. Louis*. Warner asked Minelli what the story was about. The answer was, "Nothing." Despite that less-than-stellar pitch, this classic film was indeed made, and it turned singer/actress Judy Garland into an even bigger star than she was already.

The movie centers on a family living in St. Louis at the turn of the twentieth century and spans a year in their lives as they deal with romance, childhood pranks, family relationships, career change, and growing up.

Is there an actual plot? Yes. The protagonist and her older sister are trying to land marriage proposals from the boys they love. There is the subplot of their father accepting a new position in New York that will uproot the family right after Christmas and how this upheaval stresses the entire family. There is an even smaller subplot where the two older sisters hatch a plot to sabotage a visiting debutante they dislike, only to learn they're wrong just in time to make amends.

As Minelli said, it's a movie about nothing, yet it has endured because it's a movie about everything. Almost everyone in the movie grows or changes. From five-year-old Tootie—youngest member of the family and an absolute scene-stealer—to Grandpa, so wise and yet so young at heart, each character is a charmer with a distinctive personality.

Conversely, there are stories that are predominately plot. Action-adventure novels, action thrillers, and military fiction are some of the principal genres that shove danger ahead of character development. The focus is usually on peril, rising stakes, and struggles to complete the mission. John Sandford's *Prey* series of crime thrillers expends minimal effort on emotional insights or character development; instead, these books revolve around criminals willing to commit heinous acts of violence and brutality for shockingly banal reasons. The authorities run intense manhunts to track these crooks, corner them, trap them, and often kill them. Justice is dispensed. And Sandford knows how to escalate story intensity, suspense levels, and pacing to keep the pages turning quickly. Downtime for his protagonist Lucas Davenport usually results in character boredom rather than much—if any—soul-searching.

Legendary director Alfred Hitchcock serves up a taut plot in his 1951 thriller, *Strangers on a Train.* Tennis player Guy Haines is on his way to a tournament when an intense fellow passenger named Bruno forces a conversation with him. Bruno knows far too much about him. Guy is struggling to obtain a divorce from his wife, while she is toying with him and refusing to sign the papers. Bruno is a psychopath with serious father issues, and he wants his father to die. Bruno offers to kill Guy's wife if he will in turn kill Bruno's father. Horrified by this creep, Guy tries to get away from Bruno, but Bruno won't give up or go away.

The plot is simple but a nail biter, with rising stakes and an ever-tightening web of danger closing around Guy. The focus is very much on the plot and the struggle of a normal protagonist to get away from the madman that's latched onto him.

While these examples fall on opposite ends of the scale, for most fiction it's a matter of balance. Unless you're writing a very specific genre that commands fast story action to the exclusion of almost any character development, the best action plots originate from within their characters, especially from their flaws, concerns, and desires.

In John Sandford's 2017 thriller novel, *Golden Prey*, the story begins when the villain chooses to rob a drug cartel to gain quick cash. The consequences of that decision ripple through the book. The drug cartel's thugs are sent to hunt down the thief and recover the money. And the protagonist wants to catch—and stop—all these crooks. The clashing goals of these three factions drive characters to steal, kill, cheat, lie, hunt, outwit, and maneuver. Those actions constitute the plot and subplots.

Characters drive plot. Or, to express it another way, plot originates from character goals that are acted upon. When those goals clash, your plot kicks into gear.

While this book isn't dealing with character design, we need to consider the story roles briefly in terms of how each character generates plot. Within the Fiction Formula, there exists a hierarchy of importance among character roles. They are not all created equal, yet within each role's parameters characters can bring a tremendous value to your story and the plot's progress.

Story Roles

Roles can be divided into the following categories: primary roles, secondary roles, and minor roles. Let's examine them separately in how they affect plot.

Primary roles. There are two, the protagonist and antagonist. The primary roles are essential to plot. Without them both, you have—in effect—no story. Because of their importance, Chapters 7, 8, and 9 will explain them further.

A short story can work effectively with only these two roles in play. Short novels with a simple story line can also rely on a minimum of these two characters.

To generate plot, you must know what each of your primary characters wants. You cannot guess. You must *know*. Without this critical information, your plot cannot plausibly develop.

Novice writers frequently stumble here. Even if you don't grasp the underlying writing principle that governs this point, do not ignore it. Do not slap goals on the protagonist and antagonist without realizing those goals need to connect. Elements in stories should intersect. Don't mix together random events and incidents in a misguided attempt to be exciting. Instead, link motivations and goals to actions and consequences in a logical, plausible, cause-and-effect chain of events.

Secondary roles. These comprise the supporting cast and are designed to assist each of the primary roles. They are sidekick, buddy, mentor, confidant, and love interest. While a story needn't include secondary characters, it will gain flavor from them. As a bonus, they are tremendous fun to design.

Secondary roles are flexible and adaptable. Unlike the primary roles, they can be filled by numerous characters. For example, your plot may require three sidekicks. Or there could be two love interests.

Furthermore, while you might create a separate character to fulfill each secondary role, it's possible—and often desirable—to combine roles so that a single character might play two, perhaps even three, of them. For example, your protagonist's best friend can be also his sidekick and occasional confidant. Or, your protagonist's love interest may serve as a confidant.

Combining roles is extremely effective in short stories, where the plot and cast must be compressed to a few pages.

In novels, however, you can spread out. Just remember to create roles—and fill those roles—with only the number of characters you can competently handle. The protagonist will have a supporting cast of secondary roles to help him or her. The antagonist will likewise have a posse of secondary roles.

Without them, the primary two characters can seem isolated and potentially less plausible. With them, the protagonist and antagonist take on extra dimension. After all, readers can evaluate and judge a protagonist by the friends she keeps. Who does she trust enough to confide in? Why? As for the antagonist, perhaps this character is shown doing cruel villainous deeds and seems like a spiteful, vicious, one-dimensional cartoon villain—until she is shown caring for her dog, a companion she loves intensely.

Secondary characters should be vivid and intriguing, but remember that they should not be allowed to dominate the story. As actors know, animals and children always steal the scenes they're in. That principle works the same in prose. Therefore, if you're creating fantastical critters to serve as familiars or buddies or sidekicks, take care the protagonist isn't overshadowed.

For example, Jim Hines's 2012 fantasy novel, *Libriomancer*, features a sentient creature known as a fire-spider. It's so cute, vivid, and appealing that Hines features the same creature in his goblin series, despite these books being set in different universes with different casts of characters.

Among the secondary roles, each has its own responsibility. Some of these may be obvious, but just in case they're not, I'll delineate them here.

Sidekick. This character serves as an assistant, possessing knowledge, expertise, and/or skills that will help advance whatever objectives the protagonist— or antagonist—is pursuing.

Buddy. This character is simply a companion, loyal to a primary character, and happy to come along. He can be a person, an animal, or even a mischievous pooka, such as the invisible rabbit in the 1950 film, *Harvey*.

Mentor. This character is a teacher or coach, intended to train a primary character in some capacity. The mentor is usually wise, thus fulfilling the archetype role of wise old man or wise old woman, and often bestows a gift on the primary character. Examples include the fairy godmother giving Cinderella a dress, glass slippers, and a coach to attend the ball; Obi-Wan Kenobi giving Luke

Skywalker his father's lightsaber; Dumbledore giving Harry Potter key information at critical moments.

Mentors can sometimes be adversarial, disguising themselves as an antagonist until the protagonist comes up to speed. An example of this would be the drill sergeant in the 1982 film, *An Officer and a Gentleman.*

Confidant. This character is a listener and may or may not give advice. This story role serves as a sounding board and listens to the protagonist venting, expressing doubts, and de-stressing. Often the antagonist will also have a confidant, which helps convey more character complexity to readers. Antagonists often devise the next phase of their nefarious plan while talking to their confidants.

Love interest. This is the individual loved by a primary role. This character should be worthy of that affection and devotion, and therefore should be appealing and sympathetic.

In love triangles, the protagonist and antagonist may care for the same individual, thus creating considerable conflict for all concerned.

Minor roles. In this third category of story roles, the minor players are the extras that appear briefly. Their purpose is to supply information, perform tasks in the background, deliver packages containing magical gifts, or to serve in an army of minions. They often lack names. They may or may not be given lines of dialogue. You may find, as you're designing your plot, that a character labeled a minor character in your outline takes on life once you're writing your manuscript. In such cases, if this character will be a true asset to your story, you can always upgrade him or her into a secondary role.

However, take care that you don't allow yourself to be side-tracked and distracted into creating random characters that serve no plot purpose. Indulging in this activity is likely to lead you down rabbit holes that split your story's focus and become dead ends. The Fiction Formula approach strongly urges you to stick with your outline and cut any wild-card characters that don't contribute to plot advancement.

[See Chapter 6 in *Fiction Formula Plotting Practice* for exercises in creating story roles.]

Chapter 7
The Protagonist

Let's be clear about this: despite the current fad for character equality, someone in prose needs to be the star. Someone should stand out, stand up, and stand for whatever it takes to survive, succeed, and prevail. Someone should take charge of the plot. Sure, your protagonist can operate within a posse of buddies, but he should still take the spotlight and not hide within the pack. Let your protagonist be the leader.

This writing principle seems to make some young writers uncomfortable. They squirm and frown and fidget. They're reluctant to focus on a single hero. Instead, they want to imitate George R. R. Martin, with his vast array of characters in *Game of Thrones*. They tend to make their characters a group of lifelong friends, and they envision sending this group on a quest to find the magical ring/cup/sword/talisman/whatsit that will save the world. There is, naturally, the illusion of safety in numbers, but fiction plots are about danger, trouble, strife, and achievement. They shouldn't be concerned with safety, conformity, or dodging individual responsibility. Even if you are writing about a hive mentality of gigantic mutant ants, you need one ant-girl that's different, that tends to have separate opinions, and that stays in trouble as a result.

J.R.R. Tolkien understood the need for a star. Therefore, although Frodo Baggins travels with his friends, it is Frodo who finds the ring and it is Frodo who is tested the most. The spotlight is on him much of the time, and while it does shift to shine on the various subplots, the story always returns to Frodo.

As for George R. R. Martin, my strong suggestion is that before you seek to imitate him, first master your story craft. Martin was a skilled and experienced scriptwriter long before he began writing ambitious novels.

Accordingly, instead of writing about six protagonists, learn how to handle one expertly. Give that single protagonist five friends, good and true. But do not give them all equal attention and importance.

Pick your star. This choice is critical because it will directly affect the success of your plot or create numerous stumbling blocks for it. You should choose the character with the most at stake and the most to lose.

If you have six buddies, all with the same amount at stake, then you need to rethink your plan. Choose the character that appeals to you most, and add to his or her troubles. Up the stakes for this individual.

However, should you be partial to the weakest character, the one that sits in the background and observes the story action, you will meet plot holes and dead ends.

While some nineteenth-century fiction featured the observer role, this was due in part to novelists often recording a setting or situation for the benefit of readers who otherwise would never encounter it or even envision it. (This is also, incidentally, why some writers of that era wrote dialects.)

The protagonist role carries responsibilities. This character must be proactive, not passive. That means this character gets out and does things, without waiting for misfortunes to happen. This character must be smart, appealing, and sympathetic. This character must be unique, and while that unusual quality may not be evident at first, the protagonist role must be carried by an individual *capable* of becoming heroic. The potential must be there—as indeed it is in almost anyone. But what always separates the protagonist from the crowd is that this character dares to take heroic action. This character *uses* whatever he has to stand out from the herd. And in times of danger or stress, this character will not crumple.

These days, there is a real-life social practice of conformity. Teachers and coaches are expected to reward effort instead of result. Everyone is considered special, yet no individual should stand out or display more ability than others lest someone feel diminished. Everyone in music class is considered to have talent, even if a young prodigy is playing Mozart violin concertos at the age of seven while her classmates are scraping painfully through fingering exercises. Social practice dictates now that if one child wins a prize, all the children should get an equal prize. Take the prodigy away before the others develop inferiority complexes, or—worse—force the prodigy to stay in the pack and allow the group to shame the prodigy into performing poorly. If one Little League player is pitching superbly, is this child older than reported or genuinely talented? Is this child's team winning so much that the other teams become dispirited? Stop that at once. Everyone should win. No one should ever lose. Etc.

This type of social training creates a mindset contrary to classic story design which focuses on an individual and showcases that central character's story. In the real world, even children soon understand that a cloying, phony effort to make everyone special means undermining true achievement. When everyone is "special," no one is special. Winning first place becomes a hollow victory when everyone else gets a trophy, too. And over-exposure to this diminishment eventually creates apathy, where no one bothers to try.

It's important for children—and adults—to learn how to lose with grace. It's important to develop coping skills with disappointment. It's important to receive kindness and constructive criticism, while trying again and correcting mistakes. And it's important to truly win and achieve. Allowing genuine accomplishment to shine boosts that individual's confidence and sets a bar for others to emulate. Whether the others will try harder or give up depends on them.

However, classic story design still features a protagonist, and the character must stand out, the character must lead—or learn to—and the character must achieve success at the story's conclusion, or fail spectacularly. Fiction singles out an individual and examines that character—inside and outside—to see what is possible as well as what is true and false, what is honesty and deception, and by story's end, what is worthy about this character and what is dross.

This prominence does not mean the protagonist lacks friends or companions. There are story roles for sidekicks, mentors, confidants, and lovers. The protagonist need not walk alone, but the protagonist should receive the most attention and the greatest number of pages.

Furthermore, the protagonist should undergo an arc of change—a transformation—by the story's end. Remember that the definition of plot involves testing the protagonist. Therefore, this individual needs to be capable of learning from mistakes, able to grow, and willing to change.

The Larger-Than-Life Protagonist

Because fiction is dramatized entertainment and only *resembles* real life without truly being realistic, a protagonist is said to be larger than life. This means the character should be designed to stand out memorably in reader imagination. Remember: fiction is not about writing reality; it's about delivering good story that entertains readers.

Some of the ways we can make our protagonist large and memorable are by assigning him the following traits:

Goal oriented. In real life, a great many people shuffle along without setting clear goals or long-term objectives. They endure school, and following graduation they land a job. Each evening, they come home and watch TV or play video games. They haul their kids to soccer matches. They grow old, retire, and move into assisted living apartments. They may be perfectly happy, productive, and experience few regrets.

However, a story protagonist must formulate a specific, well-motivated goal—an objective intended to cope with whatever the story problem happens to be. This is the protagonist's foremost responsibility. The goal is critical because it will give your plot its direction. And many plot elements are then built upon the goal.

Remember the SPOOC—explained in Chapter 4— and how its first element is the story situation? That situation should deliver a problem to the protagonist. How will the protagonist cope with it? What does the protagonist intend to do?

By analyzing the story problem, initiating a plan to solve it, and acting on that plan, the protagonist becomes larger than life.

Heroic. What does heroism mean? Today, real people often keep quiet and avoid taking a stance lest they stand out from the crowd. It seems safer to stay unnoticed at work. Will the boss fire you for that mistake you made? Or if you've been doing well and the boss realizes it, won't she give you more work to do? Or if you sit on the front row in your college classroom and raise your hand too many times, won't the professor expect you to know all the answers and call on you more often?

The word hero originates from the Greek word for sacrifice. Therefore, the meaning of heroic is willingness to sacrifice oneself for others.

Wait! Hold on! Does that mean your protagonist must die?

Not at all.

While many protagonists end up facing a life-or-death crisis in the story climax, sometimes—depending on the genre—the story stakes are different. Your protagonist instead might be learning how to sacrifice an old grudge, or an outdated concept of self, or a toxic friend, or the fear of change. The "death" involved may be a relationship gone bad, which must be sacrificed if the protagonist is to move forward into a happier existence.

Therefore, the meaning of heroism may boil down to the willingness to take a chance, to trust, to reach out in kindness, to speak up, to defend another, to be noticed.

In the 1955 classic film *Marty*, a thirty-something man who's a bit chunky, a bit ugly, working in a small butcher shop, and living at home with his mother, seems far from hero material. His story goal is simple. He wants to find a wife and get married. But it's hard to meet nice girls. He tries to go out on Saturday nights, but he can't always land a date. His mother criticizes him for not being married already like his cousin. His female customers in his traditional Italian neighborhood criticize him for not being married at his age. His best friend criticizes him for his reluctance to ask for dates from girls that don't want to go out with him. But when Marty *does* meet the right girl—a shy, plain-faced school teacher—suddenly his best friend is mad at him and his mother doesn't like her. Marty must sacrifice his reliance on their opinions. Not until he reaches for independence and takes a chance— thus becoming quietly heroic—does he achieve happiness.

The Arc of Change

More than any other character, the protagonist should undergo some type of transformation. It may be slight. It may be internal. Or it may be extraordinary. To change involves altering one's status quo, behavior, beliefs, or attitude. In real life, change can be difficult and intimidating. Avoidance of change is why so many of us seldom alter our habits or opinions. For example, if losing weight means changing my habitual indulgence of chocolate ice cream, then my refusal to change my eating habits means I will remain pudgy.

However, in fiction, plot involves *forcing* the protagonist to change in some acknowledged way. That is why the opening of a story usually features an alteration in circumstances. It is perceived by the protagonist as threatening; the protagonist then struggles to cope with or survive the altered situation;

and in the climax the protagonist either faces what's been dreaded since the story began or agrees to sacrifice some element of the old self or former behavior to achieve survival/success/happiness.

Furthermore, it is sometimes an antagonist's refusal to change which leads to that character's downfall.

With Marty, for example, the change asked of him is to stop seeking reassurance from others and form his own opinions whether in business decisions or in finding love.

Now, are you thinking about famous characters you've read about or seen in films that *don't* change? They're out there, and some of them are successful. Off the top of my head, I can immediately name James Bond. Does he transform or reform in any of the countless Bond spy films that have been made and recycled for over fifty years? Not really.

However, I believe the producers recently have addressed this issue somewhat. Has it helped the Bond franchise? I don't know. Although I've watched Bond films since I was six years old, I don't want to learn anything about Bond's past. The Bond stories are entirely plot-driven stunt fests. I believe audiences—like myself—want to see what hair-raising cool feat Bond will pull off next. Complexity in Bond is unnecessary. Would you rather see him crippled with angst and self-doubt? I don't. Agent 007 is a gadget, a weapon, just like the gizmos supplied to him by Q. That's one reason why—like Doctor Who—Bond has survived for such a long time despite a plethora of actors playing the part.

The point is that the closer to character-driven stories you slide on the scale, the stronger and more necessary an inner arc of change. The closer to entirely plot-driven stories you go, the less important any profound change becomes. In the latter case, change may be as slight as a new—albeit temporary—relationship (typically a Bond feature) or a chance for the protagonist to share a laugh or a drink with buddies.

The Anti-Hero

The bad boy/bad girl protagonist can be such fun to create. They are less predictable and more rebellious; therefore, they intrigue us. Readers aren't sure what they'll do next and will keep turning pages to find out.

Consider the protagonist Gru from the 2010 animated film, *Despicable Me*. Gru is a thief. He delights in scaring his neighbor. He enjoys zapping the Starbuck's line with his freeze-gun so he can have his treats without waiting. And he wants to steal the moon.

Yet Gru's true nature isn't villainous. He just needs a little help in finding his better side. The film gives us hints of his potential from the start. He might jump the Starbuck's line unfairly, but he pays for his food. He might tell his neighbor a disturbing dog story, but he keeps a toothy grouch of a pet himself. And he knows the names of his minions. The flashbacks to his childhood show us his need for loving approval.

The duality of the anti-hero's design—bad masking good—is very much what makes this type of protagonist so appealing. It reassures readers that most people are redeemable, given a chance. And it serves up complexity that immediately adds depth.

[For exercises in connecting protagonist design and goal to plot events, refer to Chapter 7 of *Fiction Formula Plotting Practice*.]

Chapter 8
The Antagonist

For whatever reason, this story role currently seems to be in some danger of extinction. When I coach students, more and more of these young writers omit a villain. Yet when we discuss character design, the features and attributes my students often love most are villainous ones. I understand the allure of rebellion, and I recognize the influence of today's deconstructed genre tropes and plots. Gregory Maguire, for example, made the Wicked Witch of the West his protagonist in the 1995 book *Wicked*. And imitators have streamed along in his wake.

However, despite newbie-writer muddle and confusion, a well-plotted story *needs* an antagonist to function properly just as it needs a protagonist to star.

Do you love bad guys and villains? Do you long to make an outlaw your hero? Do you feel a stirring of rebellion against writing about some goody-goody, self-righteous, law-abiding, boring character?

Well, go ahead and indulge.

Just keep in mind that a story role and character traits are not the same thing. If you love an anti-hero operating on the wrong side of the law—like Gru from the *Despicable Me* series—then make that character your protagonist. It's perfectly fine. In fact, if that's your preference you'll write a stronger, better designed, less predictable, and more compelling protagonist because you'll have a character that *interests* you.

However, you are not excused from creating an antagonist for your anti-hero.

Huh? An antagonist for an outlaw renegade?

That's right.

Who is Gru's antagonist in *Despicable Me*?

Vector, the obnoxious young nerd that's not quite as smart as he thinks he is.

If you're going to plot successfully and plausibly by the Fiction Formula method, your stories need an opponent for the protagonist.

Always?

Yes, always.

Even if your protagonist possesses villainous traits, he or she requires opposition for the story dynamics and principles to work. Does this mean that if your protagonist is a sociopath, his nemesis must be some whacko nut-job psychopath?

Not at all.

Granted, while some crime fiction takes this path and it's faddish now to create a tormented, nearly insane, half-broken protagonist such as those novelist Thomas Harris creates, or Chelsea Cain's unstable Archie Sheridan, or even the sociopathic hero of the hit BBC television series *Sherlock*, you must take care not to fall over the precipice. It is all too easy to push extreme characters too far so that they become absurd caricatures. For example, because the writers of *Sherlock* have moved Holmes away from Arthur Conan Doyle's original construction of a highly intellectual detective with scant social skills and a tendency to overlook compassion and instead have converted him into a mad genius with a tenuous grasp of reality, the villains in the series likewise have ballooned into ridiculous monsters. Certainly, at its start, the series was clever in how it adapted and updated Doyle's stories. But as the producers have pushed the scripts to the limit and beyond in subsequent seasons, it appears the writers are disregarding the fact that not every genius-level or over-educated individual is a maniac. And coldness toward other people doesn't automatically indicate a sociopath but instead can simply point to vanity, self-conceit, and arrogance.

With a protagonist gone bad, the story antagonist can well be stuffy, pompous, and extremely law-abiding. This oppositional character—planted so firmly on the side of right, morality, and the law—will be standing directly in your anti-hero's way, intending to thwart your anti-hero's goal no matter what.

Consider the second *The Godfather* film from 1974. The protagonist is Michael Corleone, a character that's devolving steadily. His arc of change begins with him appearing to be a decent guy, but as Mario Puzo's story progresses Michael morphs into an increasingly ruthless criminal. Michael's wife, in his marital subplot, serves as its antagonist. She is his foe because she wants him to stop committing crimes, to walk away from the family business, to return to being the man she *thought* she married. She is a caring, devoted woman trying to love her husband and keep her children safe. She knows what Michael's doing is horrifyingly wrong. She wants to save him.

From motivations of decency and love, she steps into his path and confronts him. She is an antagonist, but she is not evil. He is the protagonist, but he *is* evil because he can stop his crimes and won't.

Michael has sold his soul a long time ago. He holds our sympathy because we know he's capable of redeeming himself *if he will step back*. More importantly, he fascinates and horrifies us because we want to know what terrible thing he will do next. How will he ultimately destroy himself? And can anyone stop him?

I cannot think of a better-drawn, more complex and dimensional, wrong-headed protagonist than Michael Corleone. Some authors who create anti-heroes do redeem them in the story climax, and that can be very satisfying to readers. Others, like Puzo, choose to let their anti-hero spiral into destruction.

Now, to reiterate, although Michael is villainous and increasingly awful, he plays the protagonist role.

And although his wife is good, she is an antagonist to him and what he's trying to do.

Remember that story role and personality traits are not the same thing. They don't equate.

Your protagonist can be wicked or decent. Your antagonist can be an evil villain or simply a kind and caring person that disagrees strongly with what your protagonist is trying to accomplish. I realize this point can seem confusing, but just remember each story role and what it is supposed to accomplish.

The antagonist story role exists in fiction for the following dramatic reasons:

*To thwart the objective of the protagonist.

*To create conflict within the plot.

*To sustain suspense by making the outcome uncertain.

*To test what the protagonist is made of, thereby pushing the protagonist into heroism and an arc of change.

*To keep the story from ending too soon.

*To raise the stakes.

*To intrigue and worry readers.

That's quite a lot, isn't it? This list should show you how important the antagonist story role is. Stories of any type and length should feature a well-designed opponent.

And, by the way, if you want your protagonist to be the good one and your antagonist to be the bad one, that's more than okay, too!

Motivation

What drives an opponent to become an opponent? After all, you've created a protagonist, a story character that you want very much to succeed. The protagonist is supposed to be appealing or sympathetic or at least intriguing in some way so that readers will cheer this character onward. Who, then, would want to oppose your appealing, sympathetic, and nice protagonist? Even more importantly, why?

Let's examine three examples drawn from three separate scenarios:

> 1. Why does someone want to stop the protagonist from saving the town park?
>
> 2. Why does someone want to stop the protagonist from finding a packet of old love letters?
>
> 3. Why does someone want to stop the protagonist from restoring the Holy Grail to its rightful place?

In each situation, the objective is a worthy one. Example one and example three are aimed particularly toward improving the common good. Who would oppose any of these goals?

Let's look at them again, this time from the angle of finding an entity directly opposed to them. Don't wander off into tangents or clutter your premise with side-characters that are just being officious and nosy. Concentrate on the actual antagonist standing in the hero's way.

Now, return to the three examples above:

1.   The protagonist wants to save the town park. Therefore, the antagonist must be the individual that wants to close or remove the town park. **Why?** Perhaps because he wants to build a housing development on the land.

2.   The protagonist wants to find a packet of old love letters. The antagonist wants the letters to remain hidden. **Why?** Because they contain information that threatens a secret the antagonist has kept for twenty years.

3.   The protagonist wants to restore the Holy Grail to its rightful place. The antagonist prefers to keep the Grail for herself. **Why?** She wants to draw on its power to enhance her magic.

In each of these scenarios, the goals are diametrically opposed and the motivation for opposition is clear and understandable. It is plausible, not weird.

Strengthen Your Villain

It has long been an axiom in thriller writing that the success of the book hinges on the villain. But the Fiction Formula maintains that this writing principle works for any type of fiction, from romance to fantasy/sf to mysteries to westerns. After all, if we again consider the responsibilities of the antagonist story role, it's evident that the stronger, wilier, more ruthless, and extremely determined the antagonist is, the harder the protagonist will have to try. A positive outcome becomes less certain. That, in turn, will make the plot more compelling to read.

If your antagonist is so strongly designed that your protagonist looks wan and wimpy by comparison, don't minimize your antagonist. Instead, redesign your hero.

But if your protagonist is so smart, so clever, so brawny, and so tough that he is winning every encounter against the dark forces of Evil, then you *must* strengthen your villain. Plots are better if for two-thirds to one-half of the story, your protagonist is the underdog.

Another way of saying this is to grant the advantage to the villain. Western author Louis L' Amour said that doing this gives your protagonist "the edge." That means the protagonist's back is to the wall, so he or she has no choice but to dig deeper and fight harder. It isn't until there's a challenge that our hero will take risks and find solutions.

Consider the films *The Terminator* (1984) and *Terminator 2* (1991). In the first movie, a waitress named Sarah is up against a robot assassin that's far stronger than she is. It never tires and will not stop trying to kill her while its programming remains intact. Their goals are directly opposed. It wants to kill her. She wants to live. The Terminator has the advantage by being nearly unstoppable. Its motivation is clear and easily understood: Sarah will bear a son that will destroy the machines; therefore, Sarah must be destroyed.

Initially she seems to be no match for the robot. But as she is hunted down and pressured, each test forces her to dig inside herself and grow as a person. She finds more strength of will, more determination to survive. And eventually she prevails because of her *human* intelligence.

In the sequel, *Terminator 2*, the stakes go up because the machines revamp the Terminator model and construct the T-2000, a much more dangerous and adaptable robot. This again, creates an antagonist that's stronger and has the advantage. Why is that necessary? Because Sarah has grown as a character into a very tough and determined woman, and her young son is very clever. Also, they have reprogrammed the older, outdated Terminator model to help them and protect John. Therefore, for every plausible and logical step the protagonist takes, the antagonist must continue to be stronger. Or there will not be a rousing good story with an uncertain outcome.

Activity

I've already discussed the need for an active protagonist; however, the antagonist should also be active.

The hero and villain should be maneuvering against each other most of the time. (Too much absenteeism by either of the primary roles can weaken a storyline.) These characters should each be pursuing his or her individual objectives; just remember to keep those objectives in opposition.

Neither character should sit meekly in the bleachers, observing rather than participating, or wait for the other to do something first. By keeping them both active and busy, you'll find that your plot moves more quickly and remains more compelling.

Often—although not always—the antagonist will set things in motion first by creating the protagonist's story problem or by instigating the "inciting incident" or catalyst that kicks off the plot.

In that regard, the protagonist will react to it, but from this point forward the protagonist will be acting on a strategic plan of his own.

Let's consider the 1894 adventure novel, *The Prisoner of Zenda*, by Anthony Hope. In an imaginary country called Ruritania, a young king is about to be crowned. He is spoiled and foolish, and he is hated by his older, illegitimate half-brother Michael. Consumed with jealousy, Michael plans to usurp the king by drugging his wine and preventing him from attending the coronation. Then Michael will proclaim himself regent and rule the country instead.

When the story opens, Michael is already putting his nefarious plan into motion.

The protagonist of the book is an Englishman named Rasendyll who has come to Ruritania on a fishing vacation. Rasendyll and the king meet, and Rasendyll just happens to look exactly like the king (yes, this coincidence is huge, but get over it). When the king is incapacitated by the drugged wine, his advisers persuade Rasendyll to take his majesty's place at the coronation.

Prior to agreeing to this risky plan, Rasendyll has been a passive/reactive character. He wants to fish. He'd rather not become involved in local politics. Why should he? He doesn't know or care about the villainous Michael's plan to seize the throne.

As is typical of the mythical plot progression of Joseph Campbell's *Hero's Journey*, Rasendyll is the archetype known as a "reluctant hero." However, once he agrees to impersonate the king, Rasendyll is never again passive. He is a brave, courageous, and bold man, one that uses his initiative as the difficulties mount and the stakes go up.

However, in this section we're discussing active antagonists so I'll draw another example from *The Prisoner of Zenda*. Count Rupert of Hentzau seems initially to be nothing more than Michael's henchman, yet it's soon evident that Hentzau far outstrips his employer when it comes to villainy. Michael only wants to drug the king's wine. Hentzau wants to poison it. The idea of regicide doesn't bother him, and he influences Michael to accept it. On his own initiative, Hentzau abducts the king and holds him prisoner, then tries to broker a deal with the hero Rasendyll that would betray Michael and destroy the rightful king. Hentzau is after money. He has no scruples at all. He's ruthless and constantly scheming. Michael is unable to control him. With his oily charm, impudence, and cheerful capacity for evil, Hentzau nearly steals the story. He is *never* passive but always creating more trouble. That, in turn, raises the story stakes and keeps the protagonist and other characters on their toes.

[For exercises in antagonist motivation and active strategies, refer to Chapter 8 in *Fiction Formula Plotting Practice.*]

Chapter 9
Specialty Villains

Perhaps you've been reading the previous chapter with a squint in your eye and rebellion in your heart, because you have a different type of story in mind and your antagonist can't appear in every scene for valid dramatic reasons.

Okay.

In Chapter 8, I discussed the standard antagonist, but there are certain types of story lines and certain genres of fiction that require something different.

Even in these instances, the Fiction Formula still works. If you've been worried because your antagonist or plot doesn't fit what I've discussed to this point, don't assume your plot premise is wrong.

Instead, let's address some of the variants in plotting dynamics that occur often in published fiction but which can cause new writers confusion.

Hiding the Bad Guy

The hidden villain is sometimes referred to as the "shadow archetype." In some plots—or in some genres, such as mysteries—you don't want readers to know who the antagonist is until the end. Or you might be writing a thriller and plan to unmask the villain as a plot twist in the book's center.

If so, great! Such plans are viable.

However, concealing the antagonist's identity doesn't mean that this character is absent from the story. It doesn't mean the antagonist isn't still actively working against the hero. And because the true villain is concealed, there must be a surrogate antagonist in active confrontation with the protagonist.

Consider the absentee villain in J.K. Rowling's *Harry Potter* series. Voldemort, aka He Who Must Not Be Named, usually receives a mention at the beginning of each book, and then stays off stage until the climax, when Harry faces him in a showdown. Given the story Rowling devised, it would be absurd for Harry and Voldemort to square off in every scene. In the Potter story world, Voldemort is physically weak and struggling to survive. It makes sense for him to remain out of sight.

However, although Voldemort is a hidden villain, the story and its subplots still need antagonists. Therefore, each book features a surrogate villain that works actively and sometimes openly against Harry and his friends. This is the individual that goes out and does the true villain's dirty work. Also, Harry faces antagonists such as Snape and Malfoy in subplots that entwine the central story.

While surrogate or secondary villains often remain loyal to the chief baddie, occasionally at the climax a surrogate can be appealed to and even enticed into changing sides at a key moment, thus becoming a critical ally for the protagonist. An example of this is Darth Vader in 1983's *The Return of the Jedi* when he finally surrenders to Luke's pleas for help and turns against the Emperor to save Luke's life.

In standard mystery plots, a sleuth tracks the criminal perpetrator that isn't identified until the climax. How, then, can there be any conflict between protagonist and antagonist if they aren't in each other's proximity?

Except they might be. Part of a classic mystery's appeal is knowing that the hidden villain is operating actively in the story world, while his or her identity remains unknown. Therefore, the poisoner could be the grumpy old hermit living at the bottom of the lane, or the sweet ninety-four-year-old neighbor next door with her cats and tea cups, or the saucy postal clerk, or the doleful vicar suffering from chronic depression, or the secretive school headmaster, or even the sleuth/protagonist's chief consultant in the case. Even so, no matter who the villain is, her identity as the perpetrator is concealed until the climax. This means, then, that the major source of story conflict must come from—again—a surrogate antagonist. This could well be a police officer that doesn't appreciate the private-eye protagonist nosing around.

It could be the sleuth's sidekick, who disagrees with how the investigation is being conducted. Or who doesn't like working with the protagonist on any case and resents their assigned partnership. Some of the suspects will take offense at being questioned, and will either lie or retaliate. Multiple surrogate antagonists keep a gumshoe story from bogging down, stalling, and becoming repetitive.

The Paradox of Romance

One of the biggest hurdles in putting together a heterosexual romantic plot is how to generate plausible conflict. In a narrowly focused courtship plot, if the heroine is playing the protagonist role, then the hero must be presented as the antagonist.

Although it seems counter-intuitive, this writing principle adheres to classic story design perfectly. Nor does it require the male character to act like an arrogant, chest-beating Neanderthal. Playing the antagonist story role doesn't mean he's a scoundrel, a blackguard, or a villain.

It means his story goal is in opposition to hers.

Let's examine this more closely.

In a simple genre romance story, the primary focus is on developing a committed relationship between the woman and the man. Whether that will happen is the overall story question, which is always answered at the end.

Readers *know* the book will work out happily. What they're looking for is how the courtship will develop. They read to experience the process of how that relationship will grow and solidify.

Therefore, the key plot points are for these two characters to meet, feel the sparks of attraction yet fall into conflict, and finally work out their issues so they can commit.

A writer has two options for the romance heroine/protagonist:

Option 1: She decides instantly that he is THE ONE, the man she's been looking for all her life. She will feel very attracted to him. As he grows more special in her eyes, she may even chase him a bit, flirt, dress to attract his notice, etc.

In this option, he plays the antagonist role by *resisting* being THE ONE for her. Perhaps he's not ready to settle down. Perhaps he's been burned by a past relationship that went sour. Perhaps he's focused on his career and is too much of a workaholic to want marriage.

Remember how Mr. Darcy initially scorned dancing with Eliza Bennett? He walked into that first Assembly with the intention of not liking any of the locals. He did not want to meet the young ladies. He did not want to like anyone there. He had no intention of becoming involved with anyone.

Eliza attended the Assembly to dance, to meet the newcomers to her community, and to attract the attention of a possible future husband.

To simplify it further: Eliza attended the party to find a husband. Darcy attended the party reluctantly, determined not to be caught.

Option 2: This is when the heroine meets an attractive man, but instantly decides he is *not* THE ONE. Perhaps he's her rival for a job promotion. Perhaps he's interfering with her current boyfriend. Perhaps he's dangerous or too intense for her comfort zone. Perhaps she's just escaped a rotten relationship or has a personal issue clouding her life that leaves her reluctant to become romantically involved with anyone at this stage.

In this setup, the hero plays the antagonist role by desiring her as THE ONE for him. Emotionally, he's already on his knees, so smitten by her beauty that he knows he cannot live without her. He will pursue her avidly, courting her, inviting her to dinner, bestowing gifts, etc.

In the 2016 book *Shadow Rider* by Christine Feehan, the hero Stefano sees the heroine Francesca and immediately—in his mind—claims her for his own. Problem is, Francesca has a secret past and is determined to defy him, avoid him, and resist him because of her issues.

Both options set up the romance dynamic in a way that puts the two principal characters in oppositional roles, thereby keeping sparks flying and the conflict going.

Now, this simple plot structure works fine for short stories and short books. For longer books, however, there needs to be more complexity delivered through subplots and the revelation of a hidden villain—a true antagonist—that actively works against the couple.

In romance, the hidden villain can be the third member of a love triangle, or an individual from the protagonist's past moving into the open to actively cause trouble.

When a romance novel utilizes a hidden villain, often the hero and heroine have either succumbed to their attraction for each other or they are close to working things out before the hidden villain surfaces. Then the couple can face the villain as a united pair.

There are, of course, many variations on this.

For example, if we return to Austen's *Pride and Prejudice*, the plot dynamic spins and shifts delightfully along the writing principles followed by the Fiction Formula.

Eliza sees Darcy for the first time at a neighborhood ball and finds him handsome but proud. Then she overhears him insult her, and her initial attraction flames into dislike. Darcy is indifferent to her initially, but as soon as she refuses to dance with him, he takes a second look—and likes what he sees. Her prejudice clashes often with his pride as they meet and part, meet again and part again. But as they grow better acquainted, the Wickham subplot pulls a true, hidden villain into view. Eliza is attracted to Wickham at first. She believes his lies and is flattered by his charm. However, Wickham disappears whenever Darcy visits the community and soon finds a much easier conquest in the foolish Lydia. Later, when Wickham and Lydia run away together, the emotional stakes are raised for Eliza. By then, she has come to love Darcy but very much believes her marital chances are hopeless thanks to her sister eloping with a scoundrel.

Another hidden villain appears to test Eliza in the climax. Darcy's aunt, Lady Catherine, has intended him to wed her daughter since both cousins were in their infancy. Lady Catherine's strong confrontation with Eliza proves to be the final turning point, one that tests Eliza's character, strength of will, and feelings for Darcy.

Consider also the nineteenth-century Bronte classic, *Jane Eyre*. Jane is smitten by Mr. Rochester almost at first sight. He holds his distance. His goal is to do anything but become attracted to her. Why? A little impediment called "already married." However, not until Rochester thaws and he and Jane become friends does the wife hidden in the attic begin to take an active role to thwart their love.

Yet another romance-plot variant is when the hero and heroine meet as opponents on opposite sides of an issue. This allows their feelings of attraction for each other to be more direct and less complicated; however, they are kept apart because of an external problem.

For example, let's say they are both running for the job of mayor of their community. As political opponents, they will have divergent opinions and perspectives. Or perhaps she has just inherited the beloved family farm and he's in charge of confiscating it for a new highway.

Again, in a short length, this type of issue will be sufficient to keep them apart until the end, when everything works out. However, in a longer story, the emergence of a true villain will help them unite against the more threatening foe. Shakespeare's *Romeo and Juliet* pits the hero and heroine against each other because of their families' rivalry. Once the couple unites, their foe is the family enmity.

In the 1997 James Cameron film *Titanic*, the romance is yet another version of the forbidden relationship. Once the couple commits to each other, they are pitted against Rose's mother, her fiancé, and ultimately the sinking ship.

The 1949 romantic comedy, *Adam's Rib*, depicts a couple deeply in love with each other yet separated by being on opposing sides of a legal issue. In the film, both are trial attorneys. He works for the prosecutor's office, and she is in private practice. When a housewife shoots her adulterous husband—wounding him only slightly—Adam is assigned to prosecute the case of attempted manslaughter. His wife Amanda, however, takes on the housewife's defense, adopting it as a *cause celebre* of women's rights. The trial quickly begins to affect their marriage.

[For further assistance in assessing the effectiveness of your villains and how actively they generate conflict in your stories, refer to Chapter 9 of *Fiction Formula Plotting Practice*.]

Chapter 10
Plotting from Scenes

Not every writer works well from an outline. Some writers create their stories from a sense of discovery. They enjoy the process of exploration through their characters and story worlds. They do not want to over-analyze or over-restrict their plot ahead of time.

This approach is occasionally referred to as "pantsing." Writing by the seat of your pants is a thrill. There's an element of uncertainty to it that carries risk, and risk can be appealing. And while some authors deride pantsers as amateurs, there are successful, published writers that write this way.

Whatever your opinion, it's important to understand that professional authors that do not formally outline still know what they're doing. They instinctively grasp the writing principles of classic story design and follow them naturally through their process of discovery. Most pros seldom have the leisure to blunder into dead ends that take their stories nowhere. With contracts and deadlines, they must make their ideas come to fruition as efficiently as possible.

So although they may claim they let the idea or the characters lead them, what they really mean is that they are plotting from within scenes and the consequences of those scenes. Because whether you are trained to outline ahead of time or you work through the story as you go, writers must step inside their protagonist—and any other viewpoint characters—and write the manuscript from the inside. By that, I mean write from within the heart and mind of the scene protagonist as each dramatized event unfolds.

Prose Scenes

In Chapter 1, I explained how scenes are units within a plot that dramatize the story action to showcase effort and conflict. Each scene pushes the protagonist to take greater risks, and each scene further tests the protagonist through the story's progression.

We need to be precise in how we use the term "scene" since prose, screenplay/teleplay, and video game media each sets up scene approach, utilization, and construction somewhat differently. For example, in a screenplay a scene refers technically to camera location rather than the development and resolution of a character disagreement. Therefore, in a movie, two characters might be arguing in their living room (scene 1), continue the same confrontation in their building elevator (scene 2), and finish the discussion on the sidewalk as one character exits by climbing into a cab (scene 3). This series of camera relocations gives audiences a sense of something happening. Even if the audience grows bored or impatient with the dialogue, character movement from one set to another can be visually compelling.

By contrast, a prose scene is much more static in terms of its setting. The focus is not on a camera location but instead on the viewpoint character's goal at that moment. What is the protagonist's immediate objective? How does this objective tie into the overall story goal? What motivates the protagonist to attempt this objective at *this* point in the story? Who is standing in the protagonist's way? What maneuvers, arguments, persuasions, guile, trickery, and threats will the protagonist and antagonist make against each other in this encounter? And, finally, what is the confrontation's outcome?

Because a prose scene is a dramatic unit of conflict centered on two directly opposing goals, there is little need to move the characters across various sets. They can duke it out in the living room until the argument is finished and one of them exits the apartment.

Another notable difference between screenplay and prose scenes, besides location and viewpoint, is how many people are present for the confrontation.

A script can call for numerous bystanders. These extras help fill up the camera lens. They offer color and movement behind the principal players. Their reactions and expressions as the protagonist and antagonist argue can add nuance to the situation that furthers audience comprehension of what's happening.

However, in prose, a scene is optimally designed with only two characters present. Whenever possible, the Fiction Formula strongly recommends clearing away everyone except the protagonist and antagonist. This is because bystanders tend to interrupt the conflict. Inexperienced writers often believe such interference adds to the veracity of the scene; instead, it simply disrupts, distracts, and sidetracks what's occurring. And while a movie director can control extras that draw attention away from the star, a novice writer may find it much more difficult to control opinionated sidekicks. Every change of expression, every wiggle, every head wag or raised eyebrow must be described, and doing that requires a pause in the story action.

That's disruptive.

Do it too often, and the scene loses focus. And a scene that loses focus tends to end up differently than the writer intended. Don't kid yourself into thinking this is good. This, in fact, is pantsing at its worst. It can sidetrack the scene or even the entire story.

Beware.

Now, are you thinking that you've read stories that featured scene bystanders? No doubt you have, but were those effective scenes written by an experienced author possessing the skill and discipline to control extra characters and keep them quiet *or* were the scenes broken up, muddled, and less than compelling?

By clearing your scenes of unnecessary characters, you will avoid such pitfalls. If only the protagonist and a foe are present, the scene has a vastly improved chance of remaining focused.

Scene Construction

While stories are an artistic mix of narration, dialogue, scene action, character contemplation through viewpoint, description, explanation, and twists, scene units have a structure that's been proven over many centuries to work well in advancing the plot.

Groundwork and positioning. Don't just leap into a scene without any sort of reader preparation. Doing this runs the risk of confusing some readers and irritating others. Instead, make sure readers clearly understand what's at stake, what is motivating the protagonist to take a risk, and what the protagonist specifically wants at this moment in story time.

The more at stake, the less certain or assured the protagonist is likely to be. Allow this character a sentence or two to be nervous or worried, to cling to her motivation, and to reiterate the goal. There is no need to conceal a scene goal from readers.

The Fiction Formula strongly recommends that you never start writing a scene if you do not know or understand the scene objective.

Remember also that the scene goal needs to connect plausibly to the overall intentions of the protagonist. The plot should be headed somewhere. Will this scene, and this scene objective, help the protagonist reach that destination?

Conflict. The majority of a scene's content should be comprised of conflict. Characters in agreement are not conducting scene action. There are other places where they can sit and chat agreeably, but not within a scene.

Remember that scenes feature a protagonist and an opponent. Each of them has a goal, and those two goals should be directly opposed.

If Maurice walks into his prospective father-in-law's library to ask for Solange's hand in marriage, and Papa welcomes him with open arms, a glass of brandy, and a beaming smile of approval, **we have no scene.**

However, if Maurice walks into his prospective father-in-law's library to ask for Solange's hand in marriage, and Papa picks up a loaded dueling pistol and orders Maurice out of the house while forbidding him to ever see Solange again, we have a scene. Why? Because Papa doesn't want Maurice to marry his daughter. The men's goals are directly opposed. And while Maurice can use every bit of charm and persuasiveness he possesses, Papa has no intention of relenting.

Furthermore, if you've taken the time to figure out each man's motivation before you start writing this clash of wills, your scene conflict will be much stronger. For example, if Maurice is motivated by his intense physical attraction to Solange, plus he knows that if he marries her before the waning of the full moon he has a chance to break the curse that has hampered him for years, then he's going to argue even harder. And if Papa loves Solange very much but distrusts Maurice and believes he wants to marry Solange for convenience rather than from any genuine affection for her, then this protective, loving father will not bestow his daughter's hand on Maurice.

With motivations that strong, neither man will give up easily. As a result, your dialogue will be sharper, character emotions will be stronger, and it's much more likely that one of them will go too far.

Disappointment and disaster. Scenes need to come to a definite conclusion. Don't let them falter and fade, unresolved. Don't interrupt them and never return to the point. Don't lose sight of your protagonist's goal—or worse, forget what it was.

Remember that a scene is a dramatic unit. It starts with a flourish, and it should end with a bang. Even if this metaphor seems a bit too melodramatic or theatrical for your taste, give it a chance.

Resolving scenes with failure is tough for any writer to swallow unless the writing principle at work here is clearly understood.

Unlike in a video game, where a player's avatar must succeed to advance, a prose scene is all about attempting something and falling short. Once again, this seems counter-intuitive, even objectionable, on its surface. But more is happening here than may be evident.

As I explained in Chapter 1, the whole point of a story is to test the protagonist. That test should be so difficult and strenuous that it forces the protagonist to change. In real life, successfully changing human nature or behavior is difficult. People are stubborn and set in their ways. People like to do what they like to do. They resist change, even if it would benefit them to do so. A smoker may know all the health risks, yet continue to smoke. Perhaps she is so addicted she cannot break free, or perhaps she enjoys tobacco and doesn't want to stop indulging in her after-dinner cigars every evening. And if she inherited her deceased husband's collection of prized, hand-rolled Havana cigars and believes that every time she smokes one she is visited by her dead husband's spirit, then she will not give up her ritual despite medical advice.

Also, an unwillingness to change may make Bernadette disinclined to go along when a mysterious wizard comes knocking at the door and announces that she should quit her job, abandon her home, and set out with him on an adventure that he refuses to explain.

After all, once the momentary excitement of meeting a genuine wizard wears off, Bernadette can't help but become practical and dubious. Does she *really* want to quit her job? Sure, she'd love to tell her boss to take a jump, but she needs the income. She has credit card debt, monthly expenses, and student loans to pay off. Jobs are hard to come by. She can't afford to quit on a whim. And if she abandons her home, what about the rent payment? What about her new television that she just bought and that extended cable subscription that allows her to watch the NFL channel? And who will feed her cat while she's gone? The wizard hasn't said how long she'll be away. Who will collect her mail? Is she coming back? Whoa! There's a thought. Who is this dude with the long gray beard anyway? He smells weird. He looks weird. He talks weird. And Bernadette is beginning to suspect that he might lead her into mortal danger. She could die. That would be a bummer. Maybe she'd better turn him down and stay home.

Humans have survived a long time by being clever, ruthless, and keen on survival. After all, if it looks like a tiger den, and it smells like a tiger den, and you can hear tigers roaring deep inside it, why would you walk in there unarmed?

Nope. Better to stay out, stay away, and stay home.

This caution, this avoidance of risk, this prudence generates what we call the reluctant hero. In other words, at the story's opening, the situation should be dire enough to kick the protagonist through the reluctance barrier. Once past that threshold, there is adventure or involvement aplenty.

That means part of a story's arc of change for the protagonist, as I've already explained, is moving this character away from being cautious and prudent into becoming heroic in some way. And becoming heroic means being willing to take risks.

Even confronting another person in an argument is perceived by some folks as a huge risk. Conflict is unpleasant. In real life, it's natural to avoid it. Yet fiction won't let a character escape strife and confrontation. Fiction—through its progression of scenes, conflict, and trouble—forces protagonists to face tougher challenges.

Yet conflict alone isn't enough to compel change within a character. It's a scene's outcome that leads to change. When scenes end in the protagonist's failure or partial failure to achieve the objective, the consequences are as follows: remaining options narrow; a pressured protagonist becomes willing to take a bigger risk; the story's climactic outcome is delayed.

Let's address the last one first. Why do we want to delay the climax? Why do we spin out a short story over a span of twenty manuscript pages? Why do we push a novel manuscript to three-hundred or more pages? Why not get it over with quickly?

Because readers want the suspense of worrying about the outcome. Anticipating the next conflict-filled encounter makes them worry and stay involved. Delaying the outcome creates entertainment, and it's a writer's job to provide plenty of it.

To prevent wrapping up the story too soon, scenes are therefore designed to end with the protagonist *not* achieving the scene objective. As I've mentioned before, if you spend much of your leisure time playing video games you may not have developed a strong instinct for creating character failure. But this is a critical writing principle, one you need to understand in theory so you can put it into practice.

In prose, most scenes should *not* end with success. Success kills suspense, and it negates reader anticipation of story outcome.

Another reason why scenes should end with character disappointment is that disappointment forces the character to grow. What this means is that whenever the protagonist attempts a tepid, timid, or prudent plan and it goes awry, the protagonist must then attempt something a bit bolder. When that doesn't work as planned, an even bigger risk must be tried. And so on.

This process of attempt and fail, attempt and partially fail, attempt and hit even greater trouble, etc. as each scene unfolds then serves to create gradual but plausible change in our protagonist. To illustrate, think of how an athlete builds muscle strength. Not by attempting an overhead press of several-hundred pounds the first day in the gym, but through slowly lifting a small amount of weight, then adding a little more to it, then a little more, and so on.

Now, what will keep your protagonist going in the face of all this disaster, calamity, and failure? None of us enjoys goof-ups, disappointment, or humiliation. Why should we inflict such things on our protagonist? Also, if your protagonist keeps throwing himself at a brick wall of opposition and getting nowhere, isn't that going to make the character seem foolish? And won't a dumb doofus protagonist lose reader sympathy?

It can, if handled incorrectly by a writer unwilling or unable to comprehend the writing principle at work here.

Firstly, a protagonist's scenes should not go wrong because she's stupid or careless. Instead, they go wrong for her because the *antagonist* steps in, gets in the way, and actively thwarts what could have been an excellent plan.

Secondly, when the protagonist is clever and prepared, but loses a scene goal due to being outwitted, tricked, betrayed, or out-maneuvered, readers will continue to feel sympathy for the protagonist. The story should seem more compelling than ever, especially when she digs deeper and comes up with a new course of action to try.

Keeping the protagonist challenged, but still willing to re-evaluate and outwit the opponent, is what moves a plot forward. The key to this writing principle is that the protagonist adapts and forms new plans.

By contrast, when a writer does not understand the writing principle and instead blindly follows a rule of *have your protagonist fail,* the result is too many repeated, identical attempts and failures. This kind of repetition can turn off readers. If the protagonist stays at the same risk level, struggling futilely against the same opposition without any progress, the story becomes stagnant.

A strongly motivated protagonist will reassess his situation, form a new plan, and attempt bigger risks— the risks he probably avoided at the start of the story. A strongly motivated protagonist that adapts to escalating trouble is a protagonist that evolves.

The other reason we end scenes with failure or partial failure is to narrow the possible plot options. Again, this is a critical difference between how a prose plot develops and a video game's progression.

In a game, options are few at the beginning but expand as the game continues. In a story, options are plentiful at the beginning, but shrink with each scene.

When each major scene boxes in your protagonist, forces a reassessment of the plan, pushes the protagonist into bigger risk-taking, and steadily removes the available options, what is happening?

We are positioning the protagonist into a final, ultimate confrontation that will resolve the story question either positively with a victory or negatively with a loss.

In effect, we are maneuvering the protagonist into the story climax.

[For exercises in conflict and evaluation of your scene construction, refer to Chapter 10 in *Fiction Formula Plotting Practice.*]

Chapter 11
Plotting from Reactions

Scenes—as vital as they are to a story—make up only half the plot. The other half is filled by a) character reaction to how scenes end, and b) character planning of what to do next as a result.

A plot should not be a series of scenes strung together without letup. This kind of story quickly becomes frenetic, overcharged, implausible, and tiring to read. Instead, plots should feature a mixture of pacing tempos. So a fast, intense, conflict-filled scene will be followed by emotional devastation and recovery. This means bursts of action followed by rest, or fights followed by wound-licking and planning. In a story, there must be a time to recharge, to assimilate, to ponder, to solve, to question, to doubt, to grieve, to gather courage, to seek comfort or reassurance, to sleep and eat, to forge weapons, to renew motivation, to plan, and to resolve to try again.

This is sometimes known as the logic/plausibility portion of plotting. Scenes, with their excitement and conflict, tend to grab most of the limelight, but never underestimate the power of reaction in moving your story forward. Ultimately this half of the story is what enables it to make sense.

Some genres rely more heavily on reaction segments than others, namely fantasy, romance, mystery, and thriller/suspense. Children's fiction, on the other hand, features very small reaction segments that can be difficult to spot without practice. The current popularity of fiction designed for younger readers—or adults that prefer simple plots and quick pacing—has pushed reaction segments to the background. However, you still should understand the principle behind them and why they are necessary whether they are written fully or abbreviated. Traditional westerns, military fiction, and action-adventure also tend to employ brief reactions.

Whether long or short, reaction in the Fiction Formula approach requires certain components that need to be plotted in the following order to be cohesive and effective.

Emotional response. This component should be written so that it *immediately* follows a scene's conclusion. It should be a direct, connected reaction to the preceding scene's concluding setback where the protagonist's objective was *not* achieved, or not achieved without an unexpected price/complication.

If your protagonist has just attempted to reach her goal, found that goal actively thwarted, and either failed miserably or succeeded only to fall into worse trouble, how does she feel about what happened?

How do any of us feel after we've tried our hardest to accomplish a task extremely important to us but the attempt didn't come off as we'd hoped or planned?

Disappointed.
Dismayed.
Disgusted.
Despairing.
Desperate.
Angry.
Determined to continue.
Baffled.
Frustrated.
Furious.
Grieved.

These emotions are a small sampling of potential feelings your character might experience, depending on the story stakes, the story situation, and the character's personality and degree of involvement. They are all reflective of the hurt disappointment the protagonist should be experiencing.

Conversely, if your protagonist ends a scene feeling elated, happy, satisfied, content, victorious, etc., then a warning flag should be waving. These are emotional reactions that follow success.

If you recall from Chapter 10, scenes should not end with the protagonist winning the scene's goal. (At least, not until the very end of the story!) Although it is tempting to let the protagonist win now and then, be leery of this urge and resist it. Allowing your protagonist to succeed in scene after scene will soon land you in a bog of writer difficulties that will require serious, extensive rewriting to solve.

Again, I realize this seems wrong somehow, even counter-intuitive, but remember that a story exists to test its protagonist, to challenge that character and put him or her through the crucible of conflict, trouble, opposition, and treachery until the protagonist changes enough to ultimately survive, prevail, and win.

If your scenes are strong enough—meaning they contain sufficient conflict from a tough opponent and push your protagonist into deeper trouble—then the emotional component of a reaction is easy to write. If your scenes are weak, or end in victory, then the emotional reaction is a tough slog and will probably end up appearing contrived or implausible.

Should the scene be one of physical action, then the initial component of the reaction plotting unit may be one of recovery. For example, if Irmentrude struggles against Nefarious Nick on the cliff's edge before she is finally pushed into the ravine, and she plunges down through brush and roots before landing on a narrow rock ledge, she needs reaction time to catch her breath and calm down. As her terror abates, she will feel a sweep of relief. She will be glad she's survived, of course, but she remains in danger, unable to move more than a few inches on the narrow ledge. She will also become aware of numerous cuts, bruises, and abrasions. If she's been seriously injured, that should be noted and experienced through her viewpoint. Maybe she bumped her head in the fall and must overcome dizziness or blurred vision. Maybe she's dazed, still too stunned to fully realize her situation.

In such circumstances, don't rush through the recovery component. Readers need a breather, too, from the struggle in the previous scene. Remember that reaction is very much a part of the plot, and don't skimp on it.

Awareness of the dilemma. As emotions calm down, or as physical hurts abate, internalization comes into play. Have you ever noticed how hard it is to think straight when you're highly upset or furious? Strong emotions and clear thought do not exactly go together. However, once emotions fade—and they shouldn't wallow forever—it's time for your character to get on with the story.

In other words, what's going to happen next? Let's return to the plight of poor Irmentrude. She fought for her life but was pushed over the cliff. She was lucky enough to land on a ledge, but now she's hurt and still in danger of falling to her death. She might have a concussion or a broken wrist. She's cold, scared, bruised, and desperate to find safety, but now she must govern her feelings to think and plan how to extricate herself from her problem.

Sometimes, as a character realizes the magnitude of the current disaster, he may revert to the state of emotional reaction. But eventually he'll calm down and start thinking, because the story must go on. And part of finding a solution is to analyze the situation.

If your protagonist is stranded on a ledge, then the analysis will have to be done through internalization. However, if your protagonist has just been jilted at a marriage altar, for example, then other characters—especially a confidant—can be present to discuss the problem.

Occasionally, there will be a review of what just happened in the preceding scene. It won't be a lengthy flashback. Remember, you're trying to move your character forward into what will be done next. As part of that process, options will be considered, weighed, and discarded as the risks are evaluated.

What you're really doing is plotting your story in front of your reader. You are making your writer's process part of the story. And while that may worry you, be assured that readers will appreciate following a character through these stages. By having your protagonist examine a risky course of action and decide its dangers are worth braving, you are helping readers to remain engaged and sympathetic. They will accept an iffy plan because they've been made to understand how it's the only viable option to take in the circumstances.

But if you omit analysis of the dilemma, and instead simply jump your character into new action for no clear or apparent reason, readers may decide your protagonist is foolish by running too many unnecessary risks. Readers can pull away or lose interest.

Motivation is usually reinforced or even strengthened in the dilemma component. Remember that your protagonist needs to find the courage to brave a riskier attempt next time. Often a protagonist may think or say, "I know this is crazy-dangerous, but if I hang onto the rope I might have a chance to make it. I have to try anyway because my buddies are depending on me."

If your viewpoint character acknowledges the foolhardiness of a plan, readers are satisfied and usually willing to cheer the character on. But ignore that acknowledgment at *your* peril, dear writer.

Choosing new action. The process of choosing a new option helps the protagonist find renewed determination to try again. As soon as an option is selected, positioning for the next scene begins. And as soon as the protagonist *acts* on the new scene goal, opposition steps in and you're back in scene.

Therefore, as the *ending* of a scene generates an immediate, closely connected emotional reaction that leads to planning, so does the *ending* of the reaction segment launch the next scene. With understanding of this plotting principle and practice, a writer following the Fiction Formula can create a seamless flow of action and reaction, intense excitement and slow pondering, rise and fall of story action.

Even an abbreviated or interrupted reaction segment needs a minimal amount of emotion— possibly squelched for later—and a new goal. It can be accomplished in a sentence or two without seriously slowing down the story pace. When you look at children's stories, the reactions tend to cover emotion in a word or phrase, then jump to new intention with very little review or analysis in between. In an adult story, the story action may be so intense and dangerous in places that there isn't story time to plausibly sit down and let adrenaline shake out. The protagonist may have to keep moving quickly from one dangerous encounter to the next until the crisis is survived. However, whenever the reaction segment is deferred, it should still be flagged in its appropriate place, so readers know it hasn't been forgotten and will be dealt with later. And when the reaction segment does come, it will be emotionally intense, full of analysis and weighing of risky, undesirable options, and long enough to detail reaction for the two or three scenes that were jammed together.

Although most people tend to think of scenes as the forward motion of story, instead it is the reaction segment that truly propels plot advancement *despite* what happens in scenes. This is because the analysis of story problem and planning a new course of action renews the protagonist's determination to keep trying.

Through these components, written in the order I've shown in this chapter, you can build bridges between your scenes. These reaction bridges support the story with spans of logic and motivation. They show readers why a protagonist is taking risks, and they enable readers to sympathize and cheer that character on.

[For a checklist exercise in evaluating the reactions in your manuscripts, see Chapter 11 of *Fiction Formula Plotting Practice*.]

Chapter 12
Plotting Multiple Viewpoints

In a story featuring multiple viewpoints, the same plotting principles are handled exactly as if you're dealing with the single viewpoint of the protagonist.

I feel multiple viewpoints are better utilized in novellas or novels, although those lengths also work fine when written in single viewpoint. And while I have read a few short stories that adeptly employ more than one viewpoint, I strongly advise against it. I think the short story length works against the dramatic effectiveness of multiple viewpoints, as it is too easy to split a story's focus and run into difficulties in its climax. Therefore, as you read the plotting example provided in this chapter, think of it in strategic terms of longer fiction.

The key to maintaining logic and control with multiple viewpoints is adhering to the following:

*Limit the number of viewpoints you use;

*Set up each additional viewpoint as a subplot with its own beginning, middle, and ending;

*Remember that each viewpoint character becomes in turn that subplot's protagonist regardless of whatever role he or she is playing in the main storyline.

As you switch viewpoints—ideally following a hook, and what better hook than a scene ending in disaster—you leave or enter a viewpoint at the plot component that logically follows where you last featured that character perspective.

To clarify:

Let's say that Bob is the star player of the story. There will be two additional viewpoints. Erika—who is

Bob's enemy—will be the central antagonist. Mitch is Bob's sidekick. Bob and Mitch are vampire hunters. Erika is the local vampire queen's bodyguard. As a little background, let's have Bob and Erika both be enhanced humans capable of dealing with vampires, although neither are immortal. Perhaps Erika used to be Bob's hunting partner and lover. Then Erika turned to the dark side and gave her allegiance to the vampire queen for a very good reason that will be kept secret from Bob and readers until at least the story middle or possibly the climax. Currently, they hate each other.

The story begins in Bob's viewpoint. He and Mitch have laid an ambush to destroy the queen, who has left her stronghold temporarily. Her trip is supposed to be top secret, but Bob has found out through an informant. He and Mitch attack. With the element of surprise on their side, they nearly succeed. But Erika thwarts their efforts. Although several other vampires are destroyed in the fight, Erika and the queen escape. [*scene-ending failure for Bob*]

Angry by how close he came, Bob chooses to pursue them despite Mitch's protests that they should wait for reinforcements. [*Bob's reaction segment*]

They catch up with Erika, but this time she is lying in wait for them and attacks first. At the end of a fierce fight, Bob is wounded and knocked out. [*scene-ending failure for Bob*]

The viewpoint changes to Erika's perspective. [*Erika's reaction segment to ambush*] Although she protected the queen, the ambush shouldn't have occurred and the queen is angry with her. Furthermore, it means Erika has a traitor to deal with. Fuming and furious, she orders the unconscious Bob tied up and brought along as her prisoner. This decision launches a scene between Erika and her lieutenant, who protests the order because it's against the rules to bring a hunter into the hive. Erika intends to question Bob so she needs him kept alive until she can discover the informant's identity. The lieutenant, motivated by ambition to take Erika's job away from her, accuses her of still caring for Bob. He declares her to be the traitor and races ahead to tell the queen of Erika's disobedience. [*scene-ending failure for Erika*]

Erika's anger grows. In this longer reaction segment, she processes not only the scene that just happened with the lieutenant, but also some of what went wrong between her and Bob long ago. However, this review analysis should not be lengthy and it should not share all that happened when she and Bob split up. (It's too early in the story to reveal too much background. Keep readers wanting more.) Erika is *not* still in love with Bob. Her motivation for serving the queen remains as strong as ever. She's frustrated with the political bickering within the hive that holds back the vampires and keeps them from uniting against human laws that persecute them. Once her temper cools down, she turns her emotions against the unconscious Bob, intending to make him suffer even more than she originally intended before she kills him.

Now, with bigger threat raised against Bob, the viewpoint changes to Mitch's perspective. Having finished his fight with a vampire minion, Mitch has won but only barely. [*scene ending in success for Mitch but with a price*] In his reaction segment, he's spent, hurting, maybe bitten. He applies anti-vampire serum to his bite, and its effects are extremely unpleasant. Still in recovery, he staggers around the battleground and discovers that Bob is missing. Unsure whether Bob is dead or alive, Mitch must pull himself together and go after his friend. [*new goal ending Mitch's reaction segment*]

The viewpoint changes to Bob's perspective as he comes to. He is hanging in a prison cell deep beneath the queen's citadel. [*reaction segment to the fight he lost and his present predicament*] Depending on his state of health, he may have to undergo recovery or he may be able to start seeking a solution to his predicament immediately.

As you can see from this example, with each viewpoint change I have set a strong hook before switching perspectives. For variety, some of the viewpoints are introduced in reaction segments and some are in scenes. You never want to lock into a predictable pattern. Either way, whether in conflict action or contemplation, it is easy to establish a change in viewpoint clearly, sympathetically, and emotionally.

While some writers switch POV in every chapter, others prefer to follow a character for a longer segment of the story before shifting. I like to establish my central protagonist firmly over the course of three to five chapters at the start, maybe giving the story's entire opening act to my hero's perspective, before I shift. There's no set rule about this. George R. R. Martin's approach, for example, is far different. His fans don't seem to mind a bit.

Always remember that viewpoints are shifted for dramatic reasons, and not because you've become stuck or bored with a character's plotline and decide to hop to a different one.

The most valid reasons for shifting viewpoint are as follows:

1. **To follow the story**. If your protagonist is unconscious or sidelined while important story action is happening elsewhere, shift viewpoint rather than have someone drop by later and "tell" the protagonist—and readers—what has happened. Such telling has the effect of false drama. It's better to shift over to where the action is. Also, if the protagonist is present at an event, then use his or her viewpoint. When possible, keep the spotlight on your star.

2. **To raise threat.** By shifting viewpoint to the villain's perspective as she sets up a nefarious scheme or lays a trap for either the protagonist or someone the protagonist cares about, you boost story suspense and reader anticipation.

3. **To keep a character sympathetic.** Sometimes, a character's arc of change requires him or her to act coldly or reprehensibly at first. Yet if this character is to evolve or ultimately prove to be an important ally, a writer may want to enter viewpoint to show this individual's motivations. However, be very careful with Reason #3 as it can negate plot twists. For example, had J.K. Rowling entered Professor Snape's viewpoint, readers would have lost the entire delicious experience of speculating about which side he was on. Conversely, in a romance novel, where the hero is playing an antagonistic role through perhaps half or three-quarters of the plot, it's important to

share his perspective to keep him appealing and sympathetic to readers.

[For additional exercises in plotting multiple viewpoints, go to chapter 12 in *Fiction Formula Plotting Practice.*]

Chapter 13
Plotting the Finale

Supplying readers with a compelling, exciting, and emotionally cathartic ending seems almost to be a lost art in American commercial fiction. In recent years, publishers beset by their corporate owners' insistence on bottom-line success have pushed authors harder than ever into writing series books to keep readers coming back for more. And while it's possible—and desirable—for a book in a series to offer a climax without jeopardizing the next book in the adventure, not all writers have the skill or technical knowledge to pull it off. Many of them, sadly, simply stop their story with a huge hook in hopes of guaranteeing their readers' return.

Readers, of course, are wise to this blatant tactic. Some of them drop away in disgust but others do want to see how things turn out. They keep buying and reading in hopes of eventually reaching the true climax.

The showdown that resolves and answers the story question is, after all, an essential part of classic story design in western civilization. It is part of our reading heritage, part of our culture, and worthy of being preserved.

Yet today, as more stories stop, trail off, or fumble the ending, fewer good examples are published in modern commercial fiction to inspire novice writers and train them in turn.

The Fiction Formula, however, offers a solution to weak endings. Climax structure is designed to be a logical culmination of all the writing principles explained in this book. There are six elements utilized in constructing a climax. Some of them may seem hokey to you, or too old-fashioned, yet please give these writing principles a chance. They're adaptable to either a sentimental or a more cynical approach, provided your resolution metes out what your characters deserve. Once you understand climax construction principles and how they work, you will find them quite flexible.

Obligatory Showdown

In Chapter 10, I explained how scenes should end with disappointing setbacks to push the protagonist into taking larger risks and changing to meet new challenges. These setbacks also narrow the available options left to the protagonist.

What the scenes are doing, in effect, is forcing the protagonist into an ultimate confrontation with the antagonist. This showdown settles the matter. Win or lose, life or death, victory or defeat, the clash is designed to demonstrate whether the protagonist has passed her test and solved her story problem or whether she's too weak, too corrupt, or just incapable of being a true hero.

No matter how hidden the villain has been, no matter how this character has manipulated events from behind the scenes, now is the time for the central, true villain to step out from the shadows and stand face to face with the protagonist.

There can be no substitutes at this point in the story. So, in the climax of 1983's *Return of the Jedi: Episode IV,* Luke is brought face-to-face with the emperor, a much worse villain than bad-guy surrogate Darth Vader. In the climax of every Harry Potter story, Harry squares off against Voldemort.

If a story doesn't pit the hero against the real villain, it will disappoint readers. They may not realize why, but they will feel let down.

There can be other confrontations between the hero and villain during the story. There's no need to save everything for the climax. But the concluding confrontation is the most important. Here's where the masks drop, the deceptions end, and all intermediaries step aside for the two principal roles to square off.

Today, writers can race to a last confrontation, write a high-intensity scene, throw in special effects such as exploding bombs and raging fires, and let their protagonist stumble to last-moment safety while the burning building collapses on top of the villain. In a modern, high-action movie, such a climax is possibly sufficient. The audience gets a topper of all the other stunts thus far in the film and everything comes out okay. No depth or insight or inner arc of change is required. The audience, amazed or stunned by deafening sound and dazzling CGI effects, streams from the theater and chatters excitedly about all the "wow" it has just seen.

In books, however, pulling off such an ending is harder. Prose writers, unlike scriptwriters, have the botheration of dealing with viewpoint and internalization. We can't rely on technicolor and famous actors to carry the show for us. We are responsible for conveying emotions, and they're tough to deal with. We are expected to serve up an inner arc of change in our protagonist and depict it plausibly and sympathetically.

In certain types of stories, such as mysteries or thrillers, a last fight or capture can be sufficient. The protagonist is heroic enough to risk danger, say, by pulling a child from a burning building, thus potentially sacrificing his life to save another's. In Hitchcock's 1951 classic suspense film, *Strangers on a Train*, the protagonist cannot have a deeply psychological confrontation with the villain Bruno because in film, there's no internalization. Instead, Hitchcock must rely on a big climactic event. The film depicts a physical struggle between hero and villain on a merry-go-round at an amusement park. The ride is spinning out of control at a dangerous speed while children scream and horrified parents watch helplessly.

Sometimes, as in this example, resolving the danger is simply enough.

But books can offer so much more, if climax structure is understood.

The Fiction Formula utilizes six steps or processes within the climax. Each contributes to the effectiveness of the ending. They should not be jostled out of order, as one leads to the next. If one is omitted, the structure may be weakened as a result, or it may fail to reach its full dramatic potential. These steps have been proven again and again to appeal to readers. They are effective, not experimental.

Now, let's examine them one at a time:

Step #1—The Temptation of Choice

Although the protagonist begins the story at a disadvantage, scrambling to cope with a dreadful or dangerous situation and hitting opposition at every turn, somehow through courage, strength, intelligence, and grit the protagonist survives to the end. And there, despite everything the antagonist has done through two-thirds of the story, the protagonist might—in this last, final confrontation—prevail.

Therefore, faced with possible victory for the hero, the antagonist often becomes tricky by shifting tactics and offering the protagonist an easy way to achieve his goal.

Such a strategy is psychological and deceptive. It exploits the protagonist's weakness or vulnerability. And like all effective temptations, it's nearly impossible to resist.

After all, the story goal is very desirable or the protagonist wouldn't have pursued it despite conflict, danger, and challenges. The protagonist must have been powerfully motivated to persevere. Now, at long last, the antagonist is trying to negotiate a deal.

An alliance is offered. A deal is proposed. The antagonist suddenly puts on a mask of pretended friendship and promises to step aside and let the protagonist win the objective.

But at a cost.

There is always a catch to this offer. *Always.*

It should never be easy. The price is never low.

"Don't tell the banking auditors about the missing funds," the antagonist whispers. "Keep quiet when I tell them it's a software glitch that we're repairing. Don't say what you know. Just be silent. You don't have to lie. Just keep your mouth shut and let me talk. If you cooperate, I'll give you the money for your daughter's leukemia treatments."

Now, in this example, do you see how the protagonist is caught? Her daughter is extremely ill. Insurance will not cover all the child's escalating costs. The mother is desperate and yet her conscience or ethics are on the line as well. What if—when she was a child—her father went to prison for fraud and she was mocked and teased at school? She grew up in shame, vowing that she would never follow in Dad's footsteps.

Now, in this situation, we are balancing her child's survival against this woman's complicity in an illegal act of embezzlement and fraud.

Cruelly, the antagonist has put her in an emotional vise and is squeezing hard.

There is no easy choice for this woman.

The climactic choice shouldn't be easy. That's what I mean by the villain pushing the protagonist's most vulnerable button.

In Sidney Sheldon's 1980 thriller novel, *Rage of Angels*, the protagonist Jennifer Parker is portrayed at the story's beginning as an idealistic prosecuting attorney. Her strongest ambition initially is to put mafia dons behind bars. But her arc of change across the story is not a positive one. Instead, she devolves gradually until she loses her way, loses her ethics, loses everyone she loves, and loses her career.

The turning point in her downfall happens when her little boy is kidnapped by a sicko threatening to torture and kill him. The protagonist seeks help from the police and FBI, but when they are unable to find her child she turns in desperation to the local mob boss for help. He saves her child. But his price is the loss of her soul and ethics because he insists she work for him. She pays his price and makes her deal with the devil. What mother could withstand such an awful choice? Yet at the book's climax, her decisions lead to her defeat and destruction. Thematically the book demonstrates the adage that two wrongs never make a right.

Here's another example: "I'll let the hostages go, but you'll stay here," the antagonist says. "Your life for theirs."

Or: "Hand over the chemical formula," the antagonist demands. "Or I'll shoot you here and now."

Sometimes, the antagonist simply threatens to instigate whatever the protagonist most fears unless cooperation is given.

Step #2—Surrendering the Goal

After all the long, sustained effort to reach the story's objective, the cost of the villain's deal should be too high for the hero to pay. Have you ever gone after something you truly wanted, only to realize after your best efforts that you just couldn't achieve it?

In William Styron's 1979 novel, *Sophie's Choice*, a woman with two children is forced by the Gestapo during World War II to make a horrific decision before she enters Auschwitz. She must keep one child with her and send the other away. One child will die; the other will be given a chance to live. How does she choose? Which one will she favor? The cruelty of the Gestapo in forcing such a decision on a loving mother is unimaginable.

At your story's climax, surrendering the goal should be a rotten, heartbreaking choice. Somehow your protagonist must find the inner strength to resist temptation. This is done by utilizing what is called a "barrier of principle."

If a life is not at stake, then this moral barrier needs to provide an ethical line that the protagonist cannot cross. It may be a religious barrier, the person's conscience, cultural training, moral convictions, or simply the code this protagonist lives by. Psychologically, it connects to the protagonist's self-concept and personal ideals.

The more this choice can test such qualities, the stronger your plot will become. Readers will be caught in the suspense of wondering how and what the hero will decide.

Is a cancer-stricken child going to be denied the health care she desperately needs so her mother won't break the law? Which is more important to the protagonist? Some people don't care a green bean for the law. There is no barrier of principle to stop them crossing the line into crime. Others, such as the bank officer in my previous example, would be unwilling to lie and risk prison. Or, perhaps they simply dislike and distrust the villain so much they can't cooperate; they *won't* cooperate.

Will your hero hang onto a secret chemical formula and face death at the hands of terrorists to stop a poisonous gas being released into the population, or will he value his life over the safety of countless people?

Will your hero agree to be the substitute prisoner for other hostages? Some people—such as combat soldiers, police officers, and firemen—are psychologically able to sacrifice their safety for others; some are not. Maybe your hero is terrified, but can't bear to be thought a coward by his coworkers and so agrees to become the hostage.

The Greek root word for hero means sacrifice. Therefore, if your protagonist is going to finalize her arc of change and become heroic, then surrendering the story goal because of a barrier of principle is a necessary dramatic strategy.

At this point, the protagonist should appear to be going down in flames. This test is so tough that it will force the protagonist to change, to face old fears and doubts, to find courage, to step up, to become a hero, and to reveal his or her true inner character.

If instead your protagonist instead races to the end of your story, never experiences a pang of self-doubt, and defeats the antagonist quickly and easily, you will have written a flat, disappointing finish no matter how much action or stunts you throw in.

I realize that as you read this, you're probably experiencing plenty of doubt. After all, how can I urge you to make the protagonist fail yet again? Could this be any more of a bummer?

Bear with me. This apparent defeat through a sacrificial decision is part of setting up an emotional catharsis for readers. The key word is *apparent*. We are tricking readers into thinking all is lost, but our job in plotting this intricate structure is by no means finished. The story is not done at this stage and should never stop here.

Step #3—Burning Bridges

Having made a difficult sacrificial decision, the hero has even more to do. Action must be taken that leaves the hero no way to back out.

Nailing the coffin may appear as a verbal refusal to strike a deal with the villain. It may involve pulling out a phone and dialing the authorities. It may mean destroying the formula so that death is certain. It may be giving a sidekick the magical key that will provide only one individual with escape from the dragon's lair.

Forming a noble intention is not enough. It must be acted upon so the doom that's been threatened will come down. In this stage of story climax, the hero is calling the villain's bluff. Without the protagonist's action, no reader can be certain he won't lose his nerve at the last moment and renege on heroism.

Step #5—Wallowing in the Pit of Despair

We have now entered the lowest point of a story. The situation cannot grow worse. The goal is lost. The antagonist has won. The protagonist, defeated and possibly alone, is finished.

Your readers have read page after page; they have worried about your protagonist, booed your antagonist, cheered your protagonist onward, and possibly burned dinner trying to finish reading another chapter before putting the story down.

And now, this is what you do to them? Yes!

If you do your writing job well, the Fiction Formula assures you that readers will love it.

This darkest hour of your protagonist's life is in fact the point of supreme suspense in your story. It's what readers pay you for.

Symbolically it represents the death of the story goal. And although character self-pity is rarely appealing to readers, the doubt, angst, worry, and fear now churning inside your protagonist *should not be rushed.*

Draw out the agony of defeat.

Develop it all you can. Work it. Don't skip it or cheat readers by writing around it.

This dark moment is critical to the success of your climax and plot. I cannot over-stress its importance.

Think about the original *Star Wars* film from 1977, the very first one George Lucas brought to the big screen. Think about the very first time you saw it. Think about when Luke and his friends are in the garbage hold and Luke is pulled into the water by those tentacles. (Yes, I realize this isn't the story climax, but bear with me.)

Remember how Luke thrashes and struggles? Remember how he is jerked under the water and how tense you felt as you watched? Was he going to drown? Naw, the hero is never killed. Sure enough, just as you reassure yourself, up he pops, gasping for air and floundering. But then a tentacle pulls him under again. And again. The icky water heaves and bubbles before all is still.

Very still.

How can Luke be dead?

You didn't want to believe it, but finally you had to.

George Lucas shows masterful direction of that scene by letting the quiet and silence stretch long enough for his audience to absorb the shock, to believe that the unthinkable has occurred, that the young protagonist—the *star*—has died. Lucas waits for that emotional response in his audience before letting Luke pop to the surface again, victorious and okay.

Do you remember how elated or relieved you felt at his survival?

If Lucas had rushed the "death," Luke's emergence would have been humdrum and flat. Instead, it's a rush for any first-time viewer that just possibly has never heard about this story event.

Therefore, to follow the same dramatic principle, when you're writing prose, your protagonist needs to sit in the Pit of Despair long enough for your readers to worry that the story isn't going to work out right. We need readers to hope yet we also need readers to feel concern, doubt, dismay, and worry; otherwise, the step that comes next won't work properly.

[For additional help in understanding story climax, refer to Chapters 13 and 14 of *Fiction Formula Plotting Practice*.]

Chapter 14
Wrapping It Up

Did it concern you that I broke to a new chapter, leaving the protagonist in despair? Did you think I was persuading you to write a rotten, bleak ending?

Not at all!

I was following good story tactics by ending the previous chapter with a hook. Chapter 13 deals with only half of climax structure and how to take a protagonist down the slope to rock bottom.

Sometimes, the choice is quick. Other times, it's agonizing. Sometimes, the desperate darkness of apparent defeat engulfs an entire book chapter. Other times, it's handled with only a pair of adept sentences.

But whether short or long, the climax still has two essential steps to complete before it is finished.

Step #5—Reversing Disaster

If your protagonist has struggled, has overcome all sorts of obstacles and challenges, has persevered, has tried his best, has made amends, has helped others, and deserves to win—there will be a reversal at this stage.

Bringing this off plausibly can be challenging to do. After all, readers know instinctively that a reversal should happen. They're expecting it.

That expectation is why putting your protagonist through such a dark moment is so necessary. Readers expect a happy ending and a victory. It's up to you to make them think that might not happen.

Before it does.

The ancient Greeks had it easiest because their playwrights could use a *deus ex machina* to create a reversal. A statue of Zeus or some other god rolled onstage and saved the beleaguered protagonist. Such a relief. Audiences cheered and applauded, and all was well.

Centuries later, in early American cinema, this saved-in-the-nick-of-time solution was still in use. The 1939 western, *Stagecoach*, directed by John Ford and starring a young John Wayne, is notable chiefly for two elements—an excellent plot and what is still considered the most dangerous stunt ever put in a movie. (The leap from the top of the coach onto the backs of galloping horses.) If you're thinking, yeah, yeah, I've seen that stunt done plenty of times in old movies, that's because *Stagecoach* did it first and imitators followed. And unless it's now done with CGI, it's still incredibly dangerous.

As for the plot, the Fiction Formula highly recommends this movie as a model—up until the cavalry arrives just before John Carradine fires his last bullet—and then it's *deus ex machina* in play again. However, this movie's success and popularity insured that the cavalry came to the rescue again and again through decades of subsequent movie westerns and television shows.

When the studio system crumbled in Hollywood in the 1950s and '60s, films came under the control of directors, scripts changed, and audiences grew increasingly story-savvy and jaded.

Today, writers cannot use the cavalry—or the FBI—or the Marines—or the Men in Black—to arrive just in time to save the protagonist from an awful fate. And, gosh darn it, that makes the climax reversal much harder to do.

Your protagonist cannot be rescued. Your protagonist must save herself just before rescue shows up. This plotting requirement means many a rewrite, many a rethink, and much pacing the floor.

These days, if the cops burst through the door, it's because your protagonist is wearing a wire and has ventured deep into the villain's lair and is facing death while stalling the villain long enough for the police officers to arrive.

A successful reversal is all about sagacious planting in the story for how the protagonist can turn the tables on the antagonist. It can't be a cheat, but it should be unexpected and surprising to readers. Then, as they recover from their surprise and think it over, they realize where the hints came in your story. A clumsy writer may telegraph too much in planting those hints, but a skilled writer will make readers miss their significance while still playing fair. It's not easy to do. It takes practice, good story sense, and a little dramatic flair.

Step #6—Poetic Justice

While the climax reversal answers the story question with a resounding yes, and the protagonist wins after all, there is still one last plot requirement.

The dispensing of poetic justice is all about giving your characters what they deserve. Rewards, success, and happiness, **or** punishment, failure, and defeat. The protagonist should get the first three, and the antagonist in some measure receives the last three.

Generally, commercial fiction endeavors to supply either a happy or a positive, satisfactory ending to stories. One of genre fiction's obligations is to be fair to the characters.

It's all a matter of degree. Depending on the protagonist's effort, courage, achievement, and extent of change, the story goal is accomplished plus there may be extra rewards. Love may be won, for example. A job promotion may come. A new house, new car, or new boat arrives to replace one destroyed in the story's events. A new kitten or puppy joins the family. And so on.

However, if the protagonist tries hard but makes some serious mistakes along the course of the story, the goal may be achieved but no extra rewards come with it. For example, love may be lost. Or the protagonist survives the crisis but loses his property.

As for the antagonist, if this character was an evil villain, then he or she will lose the story goal *plus* receive punishment as death, or arrest, or loss of freedom, or loss of business, or loss of fortune, etc. Whatever the villain values most is taken away.

If the antagonist was a strong foe but not evil, then perhaps this character will only lose the story goal but be allowed to escape without additional punishment.

Even secondary characters deserve poetic justice. For example, in the 1939 film, *The Wizard of Oz*, the wizard grants rewards to Dorothy's companions. Scarecrow receives a diploma. The Tin Woodsman is given a heart.

Ending a Series Book

As I've already mentioned, stopping a book in a series with a cliffhanger just to entice readers to buy the next installment is frustrating chiefly because it doesn't play out the emotional catharsis so necessary to good plotting. Throughout the story, readers are hooked by plot twists, or the protagonist's predicament, or kept in suspense as to the outcome— but what if there's no outcome?

To avoid doing this to your readers, remember that when you're writing a series you're juggling two story questions: the individual book's question or outcome and the series' question or outcome.

If you keep this in mind, especially as you plot your working outline, you won't be as tempted to abruptly break off the story in an awkward place and leave it hanging unresolved.

Therefore, always strive to answer the book's story question. You can leave a couple of the secondary plotlines dangling, and the series question will continue as a strong hook to the next installment. This way, should your project be dropped partway by your publisher or you never finish the series, at least each existing volume will be self-contained and cathartic.

[For a checklist to guide you in evaluating your climax, see Chapter 14 of *Fiction Formula Plotting Practice.*]

Chapter 15
Advanced Plotting

WARNING: *Until you've mastered the basic plotting concepts explained elsewhere in this book, do not delve into this chapter.*

The modern world is a place of contradictions. While more American readers seem to gravitate toward reading young adult and teen stories—which serve clear plots and simplified, streamlined situations—more editors seem to be objecting to straightforward, linear plotting such as the Fiction Formula has explained in this book.

Is this a contradiction or a dichotomy? If the latter, then the decline of traditional publishing houses may be due as much to editors losing touch with what readers want as to rising competition from independent, online publishing.

My intent in this chapter is neither to debate nor speculate. Instead I want to explain what nonlinear plotting requires of modern writers and how to tackle this challenge without violating proven writing principles.

In the previous fourteen chapters, the Fiction Formula has laid out classic plotting methods and techniques that have been used in western civilization for centuries. There are other ways of structuring stories, certainly, but classic design is the foundation and touchstone for all other methods, including nonlinear.

A recent example of advanced, nonlinear, unpredictable plotting would be thriller author David

Morrell's 2013 novel, *Murder as a Fine Art*. The book employs dangerous action, shocks, numerous viewpoints, shifts in character time and place, conventional third-person viewpoint, occasional sections of first-person viewpoint through diary entries, and author-omniscient narration. Morrell has attempted to combine modern and nineteenth-century writing styles. He has followed his story cinematically while dipping into older traditions. He has also given his positive characters equal attention—thus satisfying the multiple-protagonist trend that is so current—while still clinging to a clear story question. This is not an easy feat to pull off.

The 2011 mainstream women's novel, *Emily and Einstein*, by Linda Francis Lee, is nonlinear in how it smoothly meshes flashbacks and character memories with the ongoing plot.

Trendy Plotting

Perhaps the chief editorial objection to classic linear plotting these days is its so-called predictability. Why is this? Do some authors use it clumsily? Or have we been exposed to its structure for so many centuries we're simply tired of it?

Whereas in the nineteenth century certain people might have been exposed to less than a dozen novels in their lifetime—if even that many—today we grow up saturated with stories. We are bombarded constantly with myriad forms of entertainment, from video games to television reality programs to motion pictures to books to comics to anime. Car dealerships, medical clinics, hospitals, and restaurants hang multiple big-screen televisions on their walls lest people who are waiting spend even a few moments without visual entertainment. Twenty-first-century children have

DVD players to occupy them in the car instead of staring out the windows and using their imaginations to alleviate boredom—or throwing sippy cups at each other. Story over-exposure makes it increasingly problematic for writers to generate anything that hasn't been done, or seen, before.

In commercial fiction, the key tropes that make one genre distinctive from the others and beloved of its fans are soon worn threadbare from sheer overuse. Plot prototypes become stereotypes, then clichés.

Presently, the push to intrigue or excite an ever more jaded readership causes some modern writers with next-to-no grounding in the principles of classic story design to throw together a mish-mash of viewpoints and rely on shock to handle the rest. The trouble with over-reliance on shock value is that it cannot substitute for solid plotting, and therefore it must be always topped with bigger and bigger shocks. The result can become campy, ludicrous, or disturbing.

Pressure from social agendas seeking gender equality has created the current dual-protagonist fad in young adult fiction, whereby a boy and a girl are given equal attention from separate plotlines of equal importance and with equal amounts of viewpoint. Even when the characters and plots converge halfway through, each chapter in the book alternates between the two viewpoints from start to finish in a metronomic pattern.

While the dual viewpoint structure doesn't seem to bother most young readers—presumably because they haven't been exposed yet to better-focused story methods—for mature or advanced readers, this dual structure is certainly far more predictable than any linear plotting so despised by trendy young editors.

Worse, the alternating viewpoints also split the story's focus. Dual story lines create a murky central story question. The lack of a clear, starring-role protagonist obscures the inner arc of change, lessening the potential depth and development of the character. The culmination of these compounding flaws results in an inept, clumsy, seriously skewed climax.

Writers of this type of plot structure tend to dodge the problem of how to end the book by avoiding a climax at all and not resolving the story problem. Instead, they set a hook to force readers to buy their next installment. While the trilogy or series continues, readers will continue to buy despite the trickery, but if the series is canceled without resolution or if the trilogy concludes weakly, then readers are left disappointed.

Does this mean that I oppose featuring a strong female character and a strong male character working together toward a common goal? Not at all! Nothing in the Fiction Formula approach precludes a strong lead character and a strong second-lead character. They can each pursue highly motivated, powerful goals. They can each be dimensional enough to need inner change. They can—and should—each have vivid perspectives when the story shifts to their viewpoint. But all of this can be accomplished through the hierarchy of a star character and a subplot character without diminishing the worth of either.

In my 2000 fantasy trilogy, *The Sword, The Ring,* and *The Chalice*, my star protagonist role is given to a young male character. But I also created a very strong female role. In the central storyline, she serves as a sidekick and love interest. When I shift to her viewpoint from time to time, she becomes the dynamic protagonist of *her* subplot. An additional female character, also playing the role of love interest and very much a secondary character, later became the starring lead of her own spin-off series of books, beginning with 2002's *The Queen's Gambit*.

Adept juggling of multiple viewpoints and subplots among a group of buddies is possible without losing track of which character is of chief importance, then next, then next, then next, etc. There is nothing wrong with ranking characters or focusing your story on an individual. (Imagine the military if everyone was equal. Nothing would get done. Who would give orders and who would carry them out?) Fiction needs structure to accomplish its mission, which is to provide entertainment. It should not be for real-world propagandizing of someone's personal/political/social agenda.

I find it ironic that the current trend to embrace a group of characters equally results far too often in no one showing much individual growth, depth, and/or advancement as a human being. When I read such fiction, I find it hard to identify or care too closely with anyone in the cast. I am kept more detached from the story. Instead of being a vicarious participant, I become merely a spectator.

Another trend of modern plotting is to rely on random chaos, shock, and coincidental adversity instead of the classic design of a goal-directed protagonist maneuvering against a goal-directed antagonist.

In the past few decades, the video-game influence on young writers has been enormous, yet a game and a prose story are two different media. They have similarities just as prose and film have similarities, but they are not structured the same. Jumping a protagonist from one crisis to another without reaction segments or without a clear antagonist at work against her is symptomatic of this fundamental misunderstanding. If you want to write game scenarios, continue to play. If you want to write prose, then play less and read more until your story sense readjusts to prose structure.

Failure to resolve the story question has been discussed in the paragraphs above and in other chapters of this book. Whether we should blame publisher pressure to keep a sure-thing series going or writer disregard for or sheer ignorance of basic writing principles, the result still creates some degree of reader disappointment. And if it's true that a book's ending encourages a reader to buy your next story, how many times can you trick and disappoint that reader before she turns to a different author or finds other entertainment besides reading?

Beware of trendy plotting. Join it at your own risk.

Skilled writers, those who have mastered writing principles and understand how and why they work, can adroitly employ advanced dramatic strategies to keep an increasingly jaded readership turning pages. Let's examine a few.

Writing Unpredictably Through Twists

Finding ways to surprise readers is part of any writer's job. We entertain through the novelty of our ideas and how well we misdirect and jolt our readers.

For example, in the 1980s novelist Sidney Sheldon's thrillers regularly topped the bestseller lists. He employed numerous techniques culled from his days as an Academy-award winning screenwriter, but he also used all sorts of unexpected plot developments that I call "stingers." You never knew when he was going to jerk you upright in your chair. Anticipation of that next electrifying twist, with no way to predict when it would happen, kept his plots unpredictable.

For more explanation of using plot twists, refer to Chapters 9 and 12, which address the hidden or off-stage villain and where this character's plan will suddenly pop into the central plotline to thwart what the protagonist is doing. Knowing what your off-stage characters are up to will help you plot twists and surprises integral to the story. You astonish the reader, but then as the reader thinks back over what's happened to this point, the story should make sense and the plot twist should seem logical.

As author and writing instructor Jack Bickham would say, make it "logical but unanticipated."

Deborah Cooke's 2011 young adult novel, *Flying Blind*, utilizes plot twists at key strategic points to surprise readers in exactly this way.

Writing Unpredictably Through Scene Placement

Although I strongly urge you to plot scenes with their reaction segments immediately following the setback failure, remember that scene-reaction-scene-reaction is a structure designed to help *you* as a writer and to keep *you* on track. For that reason, I have always encouraged novice writers to generate their plot outline and the rough draft of their manuscripts in this order, with reaction segments bridging scenes *every time*.

However, just as with creating setting research and the development of background information on your characters, what you need to *write* a story is not the same as what readers need to *read* it. Readers should never be given your rough draft or notes. They should never know as much about your characters as you do. They should never be exposed to every detail of flora, fauna, and mythology that you've invented for your imaginary world.

Writers are, in some ways, much like the Wizard of Oz. We create an illusion, then enhance it with a booming voice, special effects, and billows of green smoke. But all the while, we're working behind the curtain, using all the techniques we've got to keep our readers enthralled, filled with anticipation, and guessing.

Therefore, when revising, examine your scenes and subplots then shift their placement for optimal dramatic effect. Some scenes are bigger and more impactful than others. Are those momentous scenes jammed too closely together? Would they work better if spread apart through the manuscript? You'll need a big confrontation or plot twist in the middle of your story, but do the events that follow it top it in scale, intensity, and drama or do they dwindle in comparison?

Maybe you've cleverly had your protagonist discuss a problem with his friends, plan the next attempt to gain access to some fortress, and lay the groundwork for a big action scene to come. The reader turns the page, expecting to read that scene, but instead you've jumped ahead in the story—either to another viewpoint or to your protagonist who's been captured by the wizard's minions and is about to be sacrificed to their evil god.

Wait! *What?*

Does jumping ahead mean you skip the action scene you set up? Won't that make readers angry and disappointed?

It could, except you don't skip it. You just don't present it in the place where readers expect to read it.

This is sometimes known as the jump-ahead-then-fold-back technique. You set up for the scene, then you skip to that scene's setback and play it. As soon as readers grasp that the protagonist is in worse danger and everything is going wrong, you have set a hook.

With a strong hook in place, you then fold back to the skipped scene action and insert it, or you can make readers sweat through a viewpoint change before you come back to the previously skipped material.

For example, your protagonist has planned to infiltrate a fortress. He's made every possible preparation. He knows it will be tough and dangerous, but he and his buddies are ready to try.

Next page: the protagonist dangles, trussed hand and foot. The evil horde hoists him over the bubbling lava of the volcano pit, chanting to their pagan god. At any moment, he's going to be dropped in as a sacrifice. Just as the wizard-priest reaches for the lever, you cut back to the action scene that you jumped over and present it—not in summary, but in moment-by-moment scene action as your protagonist fights his way *into* the fortress. You stick with that dramatic action right until he's captured. Then cut back to the wizard's hand on the lever and the protagonist's current plight over the lava pit.

This is nonlinear writing at its best. It's suspenseful. It's exciting. Nothing has been skipped or left out. But you have altered the ordering of your scenes for better dramatic effect.

Such a tactic is certainly unpredictable. It will grab reader attention. It's nonlinear. Although it's surprising to readers, you remain in control of your material. Just make sure you don't overuse this tactic in a story and lessen its effectiveness.

Another tactic in scene placement strategy is to fuse two or more scenes together when the protagonist is in extreme physical danger. In such a situation, it would be implausible for the character to sit down under a tree, say, during a battle and contemplate how he feels after just having eviscerated a foe with his new magical sword. Therefore, although the reaction segments at the ending of each scene try to begin with emotional response, the sustained danger and urgency require reaction to wait.

So when employing this tactic, there should be a scene setback; then immediately emotions will flare; but the situation's continued danger means emotions are squelched; instead, new action begins. Thus, the reaction segment has been dramatically acknowledged but deferred for the time being so the next, urgent scene can unfold.

How many scenes can a cluster hold?

Two or three fully written scenes are usually sufficient. If you plan more than this, you are running the risk of overloading reader attention spans and emotional involvement. Remember that if a story event is momentous enough to warrant a scene cluster, then readers need a chance to breathe and process it just as the protagonist does.

At the end of a scene cluster, when the smoke has cleared, the danger is temporarily over, and it's plausible for the protagonist to catch her breath, then you should play a reaction segment to *the entire cluster*.

Does this further explain why you don't want too many scenes in any given cluster? Just how big of a reaction segment can you write? One that spans ten scenes—a ludicrous example—would become histrionic and too difficult to write.

With scene clusters and their reaction, you don't skip or omit. Instead, you strategically rearrange.

Writing Unpredictably Through Scene Fragmentation

Another revision tactic to use with completed scenes is to take an important one, perhaps in the story's middle or near the climax, and fragment it. Let's say you'll keep an essential exchange of dialogue between the protagonist and her buddy. Each character comments, back and forth, saying what is key to the situation. Then break away to another viewpoint, a subplot also nearing a crisis point. Break it into a vital but brief fragment of dialogue, then cut back to the first scene and insert another slice of the conflict, then cut away again.

This is a method that novelists have adapted from screenwriters. Known as cross-cutting, it can add intensity, rev up the pacing, and follow the story as multiple characters and subplots converge. The climax of Dean Koontz's 1988 thriller *Lightning* (reprinted in 2003) illustrates this method.

It's important, however, to understand how conflict maneuvers work within an intact scene so that you can break it apart effectively without losing its cohesion. You don't want to confuse your readers or yourself.

You can also break apart a scene in a different way by fragmenting it without cutting to another part of the story. Thriller writer John Sandford is a master at boiling down a high-action, very intense scene to its most essential kernel and only including that small bit of it. If you attempt this, after studying some of Sandford's novels, especially 2017's *Golden Prey*, make sure that the essence you retain does in fact advance the story.

At the risk of repetition, don't attempt scene fragments without writing the complete scene first. Master the design. Command the techniques. *Then* break the rules if you wish, but never the underlying writing principles.

[For exercises in nonlinear techniques, refer to Chapter 15 in *Fiction Formula Plotting Practice.*]

Chapter 16
Summing Up

In conclusion, my final advice to you when plotting your stories is to keep it simple. Don't try to be fancy or impress anyone. Don't overplot by entwining so many viewpoints and subplots around your central storyline that you can't keep them all straight. Know your protagonist's main goal and why an antagonist wants to thwart it, and work on your story from that central starting point one step at a time.

You can improve your plotting by adhering to basic writing principles, trying new things, and practicing. Never let fear or apprehension hold you back from what you want to do.

Remember that a story of any length is constructed one scene at a time, bridged by emotional reaction to the next scene. When you're losing your way, or when you're feeling overwhelmed, remind yourself of your central story question and stay on the path.

Plotting should be simple. Character emotions should be intense. Conflict should be far stronger than your comfort zone allows.

You can do it!

About the Author

Deborah Chester is the internationally published author of over 40 books, including *Fiction Formula Plotting Practice* and *The Fantasy Fiction Formula*. She has written in various genres, including young adult, fantasy, science fiction, historical romance, and Regency romance. Some of her bestsellers include *The Sword, The Ring,* and *The Chalice* trilogy and *The Alien Chronicles* trilogy, all published by Ace Books. For a full listing of her works, including her pseudonyms, go to www.deborahchester.com.

She is also the tenured John Crain Presidential Professor at the University of Oklahoma, where she teaches novel and short story writing in the Professional Writing department of Gaylord College of Journalism and Mass Communication.

Made in the USA
Middletown, DE
18 January 2019